# OVERTHINKING OVERRIDE

## MASTER YOUR MIND, CONQUER STRESS, AND BREAK FREE FROM ANXIETY

### SANDY R. WILLIAMS

# CONTENTS

*Introduction*                                                  7

1. THE SCIENCE OF OVERTHINKING                                  13
   The Workings of the Default Mode
   Network                                                      14
   Classical Conditioning of the Brain                          16
   From Personal Experience                                     23
   Mapping Cognitive Dissonance                                 23
   Takeaways                                                    25

2. COGNITIVE DISTORTIONS,
   DISSONANCE, AND RUMINATION                                   27
   Cognitive Distortion                                         27
   From Personal Experience                                     39
   Identifying Your Cognitive Distortion(s)                     40
   Takeaways                                                    41

3. STEP 1—APPLYING ALLEN'S INPUT
   PROCESSING TECHNIQUE FOR
   ORGANIZED FLOW                                               43
   Why Mental Organization and Decluttering
   Matters                                                      44
   Input Processing Technique                                   46
   From Personal Experience                                     59
   Chart the Input Processing Technique in
   Your Life Now!                                               60
   Takeaways                                                    61

4. STEP 2—PRIORITIZING YOUR LIFE AND
   THOUGHTS WITH EISENHOWER'S
   TECHNIQUE                                                    63
   Eisenhower's Matrix                                          64
   Setting Goals in Life                                        67
   From Personal Experience                                     75

Plotting Goals and Getting Things Done        75
Takeaways        78

5. STEP 3—USING CBT COGNITIVE
RESTRUCTURING TO RESET THOUGHT
PATTERNS        81
What Is CBT? How Can It Help?        82
From Personal Experience        98
Some Coping Thoughts        99
Takeaways        100

6. STEP 4—RATIONAL EMOTIVE THERAPY
FOR EMOTIONAL RECONSTRUCTION        101
Emotions        102
Rational Emotive Therapy (RET)        108
Using Problem-Solving to Negate the
Consequences of Irrational Feelings        109
How to Use the RET Principles        117
From Personal Experience        119
Beyond the Comfort Zone        120
Takeaways        122

7. STEP 5—AUTOGENIC TRAINING TO
MAKE ON-THE-SPOT DECISIONS        123
Emotional Intelligence        124
Autogenic Training        127
From Personal Experience        132
Body Scan Meditation        133
Takeaways        134

8. STEP 6—ADOPTING A PROACTIVE
MINDSET TO REMOVE
PROCRASTINATION        135
Proactive vs. Reactive Mindsets        136
From Personal Experience        146
Gratitude Journal        147
Takeaways        148

9. STEP 7—FINDING YOUR IKIGAI WITH
   MASLOW'S HIERARCHY OF NEEDS          149
   Self-Actualization                  150
   Ikigai                              155
   Core Values                         160
   From Personal Experience            162
   Questions to Ponder                 163
   Takeaways                           165

10. STEP 8—USING GESTALT PSYCHOLOGY
    TO REDUCE DISSONANCE AND FEAR       167
    Fear as a Part of Cognitive Dissonance  168
    Gestalt Therapy                     169
    Additional Fear Management Techniques   174
    From Personal Experience            175
    Dream Journal                       176
    Takeaways                           178

    *Conclusion*                        179
    *References*                        183

# INTRODUCTION

> *Don't get too deep, it leads to overthinking, and overthinking leads to problems that do not even exist in the first place.*

— JAYSON ENGAY

I haven't met you, perhaps, but I see you. I know you, and I feel you. You are like me, an overthinker. You always have been one, and maybe you now realize instinctively that this is keeping you from being the best version of yourself. You are most likely tired of the constant rut in which your brain keeps running. The endless loops of worry and anxiety that your mind traverses are torturous enough without also slowing down your mental faculties. You have tried and tested several methods to train your brain out of this pointless maze, and yet, they have been in vain. There are the endless, exhausting nights when you can't sleep; the opportunities missed; the rejections—personal and professional — that still gnaw at you; and your ebbing self-confidence.

First, let me tell you that you aren't alone. Studies show that seventy-three percent of people aged between twenty-five and thirty-five live with the consequences of overthinking (Santilli, 2022). This could take on the form of dwelling in the past or pondering the future. That is not all bad, is it? The problem is that overthinking is predominantly negative. It does not take into account the good things that have happened to you or the dreams that wait to unfold. It focuses instead on trying to find answers for why your life hasn't turned out the way you wanted it to and mulls over every regrettable episode that you have faced and predicts the worst possible outcome that could arise.

Do the symptoms I have mentioned above ring a bell for you? How many of the below would you check as a part and parcel of your personality or recognize as always having struggled with?

- An endless desire for perfection.
- The crushing fear of failure, rejection, and trying out anything new.
- Several opportunities that have regrettably sailed past.
- A tendency to procrastinate.

- The exhaustion of spiraling thoughts, sleepless nights, and overthinking.
- Thoughts that hurt your well-being, self-esteem or confidence.
- Poor decisions or a fear of making them.
- Self-defeating and self-limiting beliefs that stop you from doing things.
- Health problems associated with overthinking.

Though you have held it together, you probably feel that you have reached the end of your rope or that your life is unraveling without you being able to gather the threads. Let me assure you, I know exactly what you are going through because I have been there myself.

## WHY *OVERTHINKING OVERRIDE?*

*Overthink Override* is uniquely based on the experiences of its author, who, like you, spent a long time trying to control her spiraling thoughts before studying, practicing, and finding a way out of them. This book, however, is not a memoir. It has been meticulously researched to include current and scientifically proven techniques that will help you:

- understand why you overthink.
- identify the seventeen primary cognitive distortions responsible for overthinking.

- use Allen's Input Processing Technique to organize your life and thoughts.
- apply Eisenhower's Matrix for the right priorities.
- set goals the smart way for growth.
- use CBT exercises to challenge thoughts and beliefs and restructure the brain.
- employ rational emotive therapy to problem-solve and make decisions.
- find the emotional intelligence trait required through Autogenic Training.
- adopt a proactive mindset to erase procrastination.
- use Maslow's theory with Japanese philosophy to override perfectionism.
- apply Gestalt Therapy to push past cognitive dissonance and fear.

Some of the concepts and terms above could seem alien or overwhelming and straight out of a science journal, but I can vouch for their efficacy and guarantee that you can break free of your thought patterns easier than you imagine. In fact, at least a few of the techniques that I will be putting forth are techniques that celebrities no less than Kate Middleton, Madonna, Lady Gaga, and Serena Williams swear by (Graham, 2022).

Although it took several years for me to research and test the eight-step process, you can incorporate them right away. Overcoming fear and dissonance, a missing piece of the puzzle that no one else talks about, is exclusively offered here in practical terms for you to create a system that can't fail!

Ultimately, the eight steps that *Overthinking Override* provides you will ensure you can make decisions logically and without emotions involved, stop procrastination, and end the perfectionism pursuit. In addition, you will have various steps to focus on the emotional aspects to end rumination and overthinking, leading to a life where you won't miss a single opportunity again.

## MEET THE AUTHOR

Sandy R. Williams has walked in the shoes of an over-thinker. Paralyzing fears, missed opportunities, and decision paralysis once dominated her life. These not only kept her awake at night but also stagnated her personal and professional growth. It was not until she missed a career-changing opportunity because of her inability to make quick decisions that she finally realized the toll her overthinking was taking.

Taking a pragmatic approach, Sandy started questioning her own beliefs and confronting her habit of excessive rumination. At times, this introspective journey spiraled into another overthinking loop.

In this transformational guide, Sandy shares personal experiences and practical tools to break free from the grips of overthinking. Her life, post-transformation, is a testament to the power of mental liberation. With her newfound freedom, she's found happiness, established stronger relationships, achieved professional success, and secured her finances in ways she never thought possible. Today, Sandy encourages overthinkers to set themselves free from spiraling thoughts and self-limiting fears to enrich their lives, become powerful, and enjoy every moment of every day.

Before we start, here are some quick questions you can ask yourself: *Are you ready to walk through the eight steps to freedom from overthinking? Are you looking for practical answers via worksheets and exercises? Are you passionate about never missing another opportunity?*

If so, let us step right into how your mind works...

# 1

# THE SCIENCE OF OVERTHINKING

Understanding the "how" and "why" of something is necessary for finding successful workarounds. In this chapter, we look at the science behind overthinking and why certain "brain habits" can make you more prone to it. This will help you understand your situation better, even as you try to find the motivation to change the same old patterns that your brain falls into.

There is a term we often come across called "brain plasticity" (Virtanen, 2022). In layman's terms, this refers to the brain's ability to change and adjust as a result of experience. It's like the brain's way of remodeling or reorganizing itself. The more plasticity your brain has, it can create new neural networks, allowing you to think or form associations in new ways. As you might guess, neural plasticity is at its best or most active when you are younger, and though it is definitely present as you become more mature, it is not as adaptive to change.

By the time a person hits twenty-five years of age or thereabouts, the neuroplasticity of the brain solidifies, which means that new neural pathways aren't as readily created. It is also around this same time that the prefrontal cortex of the human brain, the part associated with memory retention and complex cognition, fully develops.

However, there is new research (Virtanen, 2022) that suggests that though a younger brain is more moldable, it is possible to train, learn, and adapt the brain even past the ripe old age of twenty-five. Granted, it requires more effort, but it is not impossible. However, in order to initiate changes, one must know what exists before the change. Thus, let us first look at what happens inside our brains more closely and how we can slowly work on it.

## THE WORKINGS OF THE DEFAULT MODE NETWORK

Have you ever bought a new smartphone? New smart-phones come with factory settings or a default mode. When you start using it, you get to set the phone up however you'd like. You get to pick everything from the screensaver to the font to your ringtone based on your preferences.

Similarly, the default mode network (DMN) of our brain is what pre-exists whenever our brain is not engaged in an activity. Let us quickly look at what this means and how it is ingrained in us from a very young age.

The DMN of the brain is made up of a couple of regions that are very active when the brain is in its passive or resting stage (Buckner, 2013). However, to think that these regions are activated only when the brain is at ease would be a misunderstanding of how it works. In fact, DMN also shows itself to be activated during tasks, such as recalling a past event or contemplating the future. Thus, the DMN comprises areas in the brain that are mainly responsible for patterns of cognition. In other words, when we allow our brains a free flow of ideas or to just pursue one memory or thought after another—what we term as letting the mind run free—the DMN is the part of the brain working most. The DMN is not as active when our mind is doing specific activities, such as reading or responding to stimuli around us.

Initial studies suggest that several mental diseases, such as Alzheimer's disease, dementia, schizophrenia, depression, and autism, involve a disruption of the DMN in the brain. Though it remains to be seen whether this is a cause or result of the illness.

In the next section, we see how the brain learns to associate certain sounds, smells, or visual stimuli with feelings or responses via classical conditioning.

## CLASSICAL CONDITIONING OF THE BRAIN

Classical conditioning was first observed and recorded by Russian Physiologist Ivan Pavlov, who noticed that dogs in the laboratory salivated upon seeing the people who normally brought them food, even if they did not have the food bowls with them (Stangor & Walinga, 2014). He devised an experiment where meals were preceded by a whistle every day. Initially, the dogs showed no response to the whistle. They would only start showing signs of salivation upon seeing the food brought to them. But over time, something rather strange happened. The dogs figured out that a meal always followed the whistle. Thus, they started salivating when they heard the whistle, even before they saw or smelled the food. This was termed "classical conditioning" of the brain. In other words, over time, our brain associates certain types of stimuli with not-necessarily connected objects, thoughts, or memories.

The same was true for reverse conditioning as well. When the whistle before every meal was stopped over a period of time, the dogs started salivating less when exposed to the whistle sporadically. They started disconnecting the sound from the thought of food, eventually forgetting the link between it and looking forward to their meal.

Classical conditioning was an important breakthrough in the study of the mind, which established that our external environment plays a role in the ways we attach significance to things or think about events, people, and situations. Phobias, for instance, could be explained to a large extent by classical conditioning. Certain places, people, or situations that our mind has linked to a traumatic event in the past will continue to trigger the same panic or fear in the future, even though these particular stimuli may be unconnected with the event itself. For instance, say you got locked in a closet as a child and happened to feel something crawl across your foot, which you thought of then as a spider, never actually seeing what it was. You may develop a lifelong aversion toward spiders because they remind you of the dark, cramped, closed feeling of being trapped in the closet that frightened you as a child. Similarly, Post Traumatic Stress Disorder (PTSD) is another aspect that can be explained by classical conditioning. Our brain associates something that existed at the site of the trauma with the pain, suffering, or fear of the trauma itself. For instance, suppose you were the victim of a violent car crash. The last thing you ate just before the crash could have been a couple of potato chips. Now, every time you see a bag of potato chips in the store or in someone's hands, you feel severely anxious, experiencing shortness of breath or palpitations.

With PTSD and certain forms of severe phobias, though reverse conditioning to dissociate the symbol from the trauma can be achieved, it takes more time and effort on the part of the sufferer to attain this. However, in cases where there is no trauma involved, it is possible to reverse the negative conditioning of the brain to de-link our responses from triggers or stimuli.

### Conditioning and DMN

Research shows that DMN plays a vital part in the conditioning and deconditioning of the brain (Rebello et al., 2018). The study also shows that up until between seven to nine years of age, the DMN shows no connected patterns, or rather an immaturity to process things seen or heard in a coherent fashion. However, between seven to thirteen years of age, the DMN starts to progressively function like that present in the adult brain. These changes are also connected with a rapid pace of learning from the environment, along with picking up on social cues from relationships with family members and peers. This process of maturation continues till the age of twenty-one, when the DMN is said to be fully developed.

It is also evident that childhood trauma; mental, physical, or emotional abuse; severe poverty; exposure to illness or death of loved ones and other tragic events can be funda-mental in the onset of mental illnesses later on in life. There is also reason to believe that such trauma and emotional pain are linked to both the DMN and the conditioning feature of the brain that we saw earlier. In other words, these memories and unconnected stimuli in the brain are more likely to trigger stress, anxiety, and depression in the subjects even later on in life when the causes of the trauma have been removed.

Theoretically speaking, we learn to attach memories to objects or stimuli as early as seven to nine years of age (Rebello et al., 2018). The human brain can develop negative and self-sabotaging patterns of thought very early in life. This is also why breaking free of these habits can be challenging, involving a lot of self-work.

### Conditioning and Cognitive Dissonance

Habits go a long way in the way you react to situations, people, and events. Even the stress that is part of what you experience can be a product of how your brain has been wired. Let us look at what mental dissonance is and why it is linked to the DMN and the conditioning it is habituated to.

As the DMN is a self-referential part of the brain, mostly hung up on feelings and memories about things we have already experienced or on events yet to come, it plays a crucial role in forming what I would term your "brain habits"—i.e., how you use your brain when it is resting, to reflect on what has happened and what may happen as a consequence can become a routine process. In other words, if you are a person who keeps going over events to determine your mistakes; or what people think of you; or focus on ways in which mistakes could have been avoided so that people do not think of you negatively—this can become a pattern. These types of thoughts are not constructive and will likely create a habitual rut of blame, anxiety, and depression.

Let us now turn to what cognitive dissonance means. Simply put, it is the disconnect between two contradictory points of view, feelings, or ideas that your mind can simultaneously house. Since we as a species tend to seek consistency in our actions, words, and thoughts, cognitive dissonance can become a very uncomfortable state of being. In the above case, you may try to reduce the dissonance you experience by explaining or rationalizing the mistake you made by saying, for instance, that you were drunk or that somebody provoked you. One of the easiest ways we try to come to terms with things that make us uneasy is by placing the blame and guilt we feel on an external factor (person, event, or situation), out of our control.

Cognitive dissonance can also be the nonalignment of our actions with our values or ideas. For instance, suppose you are, by nature, a truthful and honest person. But in order to meet your work targets, without which you can't get that promotion, you resort to a few underhand or ethically gray work practices. The result is that you get the promotion you had been vying for, but you also feel very guilty and depressed about it. You may be hypersensitive to questions about your eligibility for the promotion, and you might go out of your way to keep proving that you really deserved it.

## Cognitive Dissonance and Stress

Long story short, your learned mental habits can lead to cognitive dissonance, which in turn leads to stress. You may think that stress is something related to the mind, and you would be only partially right. The fact of the matter is that stress affects pretty much your entire body, right from your brain to your cells and even your organ systems (Chu et al., 2022). Stress can have harmful effects on your circulatory, respiratory, digestive, nervous, muscular, and reproductive systems.

The response to stress starts with the brain sending out signals, which prompt the release of certain hormones at the cellular level. These hormones are designed to make our body and mind able to survive better. However, if the body and mind are subjected to long-term stress, or chronic stress, then this defense mechanism becomes maladapted to protect your body. In other words, continuous stress for the body means constant production of stress hormones, which leaves your body and mind perpetually in a state of fight, flight, or freeze, the three most common responses to danger.

If you are wondering how you can recognize symptoms of stress, the following may give you an indicator:

- headaches
- frequent feelings of depression or anxiety
- insomnia

- heartburn
- rapid breathing
- palpitations or faster heart rate
- high blood sugar
- high blood pressure
- stomachache, indigestion, or nausea
- muscle tensing or rigidity
- lowered libido, missed period, or impotence

If anything is clear from the list above, it is that stress can affect every part of your body in the long run. Stress is also linked to increased chances of cardiovascular problems, breathing issues, diabetes, and obesity (Pietrangelo, 2020).

Stress can also wreak havoc on your thinking as it disrupts sleep, increases anxiety and depression, and reinforces patterns of overthinking and rumination. It can create mental fog and affect your ability to think clearly and come up with solutions to everyday problems.

So far, we have talked about how the wrong conditioning of the brain can cause cognitive dissonance, leading to stress, which can cause mental, physical, and emotional illnesses. Overthinking and rumination can ultimately result in self-destructive habits.

The following story will show how overthinking can lead to a treadmill of unproductivity.

## FROM PERSONAL EXPERIENCE

I was in charge of a fundraising event for a nonprofit organization that I worked for. I was so worried about everything going perfectly that I couldn't sleep for days. I overthought and micromanaged every detail and pushed away my colleagues' help.

The day of the event, I was exhausted and on edge. I snapped at a volunteer who had made a minor mistake, causing them to leave the event upset. My colleagues noticed my behavior and urged me to take a break, but I refused. I was determined to see the event through to the end. The event concluded without too many glitches.

Looking back, I realized that my overthinking had caused me to miss the bigger picture. The event was a success, but my behavior caused unnecessary stress and tension for many of my colleagues and volunteers.

If only my brain was trained like it is now! So, what can you do if you're in a similar situation?

## MAPPING COGNITIVE DISSONANCE

The following is a simple chart to map your cognitive dissonance every time you feel ill-at-ease in your mind or torn between conflicting thoughts or desires.

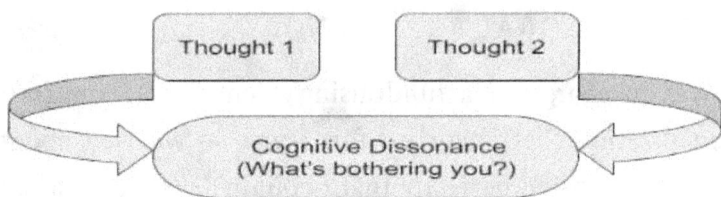

Use the boxes above to determine the thoughts that are at odds within you.

**Step 1:** Replace "Thought 1" with an idea or value that you have always believed in.

**Step 2:** "Thought 2" will be an idea, value, or action in opposition to Thought 1 that you are struggling with at the moment.

**Step 3:** Cognitive Dissonance—identify the mental discomforts that these opposing thoughts are creating (like anxiety, anger, etc.).

Repeat this exercise as many times as you want to pinpoint ideas, thoughts, and beliefs that could be making you uncomfortable.

## TAKEAWAYS

> *A world constructed from the familiar is the world in which there's nothing to learn.*
>
> — ELI PARISER

Feeling uncomfortable in situations that cause mental dissonance is a sign that you need to discover new ways, beliefs, and patterns of thinking. Otherwise, you may fall back into the negativity of rumination. In the next chapter, we will try to spot and address the distortions that cause uncomfortable feelings.

# 2

# COGNITIVE DISTORTIONS, DISSONANCE, AND RUMINATION

In the last chapter, we looked at what cognitive dissonance means and how it can lead to stress. Here we take this concept forward to look at a term that we have merely touched upon thus far—i.e., cognitive distortion and how it can lead to rumination. Before we look at the eight steps to recovery from overthinking, understanding what this term means will help toward rooting your problem in its scientific, biological, and psychological contexts.

## COGNITIVE DISTORTION

The American Psychological Association (APA) defines "cognitive distortion" as a faulty or inaccurate thought, idea, or perception about people, places, events, or situations (*Cognitive distortion*, n.d.). All of us engage in such thoughts at some point in time. In fact, they are so common that psychologists sometimes refer to them as "automatic thoughts" (Huntington, n.d.). They are one of the most normal ways in which we react to frustrating situations and are usually exaggerated, negative generalizations that we use to vent our feelings. For instance, say your partner forgot to get the groceries that you had asked them to; your first thought could be, *they are always forgetful. They never do things on time.* If you had been asked a little while ago, you might have said (more accurately) that your partner is a responsible person who occasionally, like everybody else, forgets to do things. This is just one of the many kinds of cognitive distortions possible.

The concept of cognitive distortion was born from efforts to find the link between cognition and our emotions. In fact, most psychologists would now agree that our thoughts and feelings are inextricably interrelated. Cognitive distortions are so subtle that we live without even realizing that we use these negative affirmations to get through life. Unfortunately, they are directly proportional to the occurrence of emotional and mental disorders like anxiety and depression (Ackerman, 2017b).

The problem with habitually using cognitive distortions to explain or rationalize what is happening to us is that it leads to overthinking, rumination, and cognitive dissonance, the consequences of which we have covered in the previous chapter.

Cognitive distortions can be of many types, based on the arguments and worldviews we use to make sense of or to explain away what has happened to us. In the next sections, we will examine sixteen different types of distortions (Ackerman, 2017b) and how they can pull you away from achieving mental wholeness or harmony.

### All-Or-Nothing, Black-Or-White, or Polarized Thinking

As children, we often look at the world in binaries: good/bad, white/black, light/dark, man/woman, and so on. As we grow, we realize that there are no exclusive binary opposites in the world and that most things lie in a spectrum in which the binaries make up the extremes. For instance, no person is all good or bad. Most people lie somewhere in the range between these two points. This kind of realization happens increasingly as our bodies, minds, and emotions mature and is necessary for us to "grow up" in all the senses of the term. When we refuse to look at the world in its shades of gray, there is an issue because everything is either great or horrible. By the same extension, our self-estimation can only always be "I am the best/worst," and not as it actually is — "I am good at some things, okay at others, and terrible at a few things. None of these necessarily defines me."

## *Blaming*

All of us are guilty of this at times. You would love to blame anything and anyone for something you can't do. For instance, "My report is not complete because my boss is a micromanager, my coworkers are too loud, the temperature in the office is not right…" etc. The blame game helps us to establish ourselves as victims rather than as people who did not get things done because of laziness, procrastination, or other factors. When this happens within families or relationships, with one person always blaming the other(s) for what goes wrong, then it can lead to many problems.

## *Catastrophizing/Minimization or Maximization*

Making mistakes is a part and parcel of living life. There are so many variants of the quote that goes: "If you haven't made any mistakes, you haven't tried anything new" (Quote Investigator, 2014). But what if these errors are blown out of proportion, and a person spends all their time assessing their worth based on the mistakes they make? They will often say things like, "I am no good. I am a failure. I will never learn," etc.

There is a corollary to this as well. A person who is afraid to acknowledge themselves, and their achievements will always underplay their success as a fluke or chance or ascribe it to somebody else's guidance and so on. They will continue to consider themselves as "mediocre" at whatever they undertake.

## Change Fallacy

Expecting too much of others can be burdensome not just for you but also for the person to whom you look for your "success." When you expect the world to change for you, and you can't do anything yourself to compromise or adjust to the situation, it results in a fallacy of change. For instance, you feel that your partner or significant other can be manipulated or pressured into doing your bidding or changing their behavior or ideas if you keep telling them "No" every time they want to do something you do not agree with. You think that they will learn to conform to your expectations in the future. You rationalize this expectation further by telling yourself things like, *I can be a happier and better partner only if my partner understands my needs. So, I must ensure they behave as I want them to.*

## Control Fallacies

Control fallacies can manifest themselves in two ways. Either you feel that you are on top of things, that you have absolute control over them, or you feel that things are out of your hands and that everything is spiraling out of control.

Both these are inaccurate ideas and can have damaging repercussions, because they do not truly reflect how the world works. It is true that there are many things we can control, such as how we choose to respond to things or look at events, etc. However, there are many factors out of our control as well. For instance, somebody treating us badly, without any provocation on our part, could be more a reflection of who they are than something being wrong with us. However, if you believe in the first form of control fallacy, you may attribute everything to yourself. This also includes people who believe that they can "save" others or make others "happy" in relationships.

In the second case, you are always blaming people and situations around you for everything and anything that goes wrong. You make yourself out to be the perpetual victim who is wronged, shunned, mistreated, or misjudged. For instance, your boss is mean to you, your coworkers are always gossiping about you, your parents have always put unrealistic expectations on you, your spouse never listens to you, and the list can just go on endlessly.

*Disqualifying the Positive*

This is a sense of unnecessary, acute modesty that a person can't get out of. Nothing you do is ever good enough for praise or appreciation. Despite evidence to the contrary, you continue to believe that you aren't worthy of anything. If your manager praises your work, they are just bolstering employee morale. If somebody has commented positively on your appearance, they are being kind and nothing more. The good grades you got are a reflection of the teacher's generosity. This is a very negative mentality because you fail to give yourself credit for the things you accomplish. It is often accompanied by a fear that if you acknowledge yourself, you might get too complacent or that it may lead to failure or a negative outcome.

### Emotional Reasoning

We are often told that giving validation to our feelings is a good thing. And yes, telling ourselves that our feelings are real is a way of understanding why they exist in the first place. But you can carry it too far if you think that feeling a certain way is confirmation of your worst conjectures. For instance, suppose you feel jealous every time your partner talks to their colleague or friend; you need to understand why such a feeling is triggered, especially when you are okay with them interacting with other similar friends. However, your jealousy can't be construed as concrete proof that your partner is having an affair. Not everything is what you feel about it. However, the situation could warrant having a heart-to-heart talk with your partner, especially if you feel that you are being neglected in the relationship.

## *Fairness Fallacy*

When we read children's stories, we are told of an inherently fair world where virtues are rewarded, vices are punished, good people receive justice, while the wicked are handed down a fate in accordance with their actions. If we fail to grow out of this fairy-tale take on life, it may leave us feeling extremely angry, frustrated, or sad every time something happens unaligned with this feeling of "fairness" we carry within. For one thing, "fairness" itself is something subjective. What may look fair to you need not appear so to another. For example, after working hard all year, you may think you deserve a promotion. The promotion went to someone who met a different set of criteria than what you had in mind. The circumstances could make you feel irritated, resentful, or desperate. In reality, insufficient research on your part on the promotion criteria erroneously made you believe you were entitled to it.

## *Fortune Telling, Jumping to Conclusions, or Making Assumptions*

This is when we make unfounded assumptions about what we have heard, seen, or experienced without understanding the big picture. For example, you waved at a friend who you are not even sure saw you. The friend walked on without waving back at you. Instead of admitting that you were probably too far off for them to spot, you dwell on reasons why your friend could be mad at you. This can also sometimes tend toward mind reading and assigning reasons why people may have behaved a certain way with you.

Fortune telling is exactly what it sounds like. You make up your mind to do or not to do things based on a prophecy somebody has made or you have read. This prediction is not based on any facts about your persona or a rational explanation, yet you are convinced that it is the "truth."

### Heaven's Reward Fallacy

Very closely linked to the fairness fallacy, this one also banks too much on a "larger purpose or a heavenly reward" in return for all our struggles, strife, and activities. We think that because we have been hard-working, self-sacrificing, or generous, someone will see these qualities and reward us justly in the future. When reality does not play out as per our expectations, we spiral back into feelings of anger, frustration, sadness, or despair.

It is important to understand that sometimes things do not work out, not because we did not work hard enough or because we did not deserve it, but simply because of other factors. Not seeing this can lead to unnecessary mental anguish.

## *Labeling or Mislabeling*

Labels are the tags we attach to ourselves or to others in an attempt to make sense of people and personality types. Though these can be helpful broadly speaking, you may also carry them to extremes. For instance, you may be a clumsy person. But if this is what you keep emphasizing, or constantly telling yourself and others, then that is simply the way you will continue to see yourself. What you believe of yourself will reinforce your image and personality as being clumsy.

This can happen with other people as well. If you keep calling somebody, especially somebody who is reliant on your ideas, lazy or mediocre, then they will tell themselves that and start believing they are lazy. You will never be able to see them as anything but lazy. This would also be a way for you to excuse your own problems. For instance, you would say, "I got angry and shouted at them because they were so lazy," instead of acknowledging that you lost your temper.

## *Mental Filtering*

This is when your mind sees only the negative, ignoring all the good and positives that have been a part of things. For instance, your significant other makes a statement that they do not like some particular, insignificant aspect about you. You have been with this person for years, and this is just one negative comment among many positive comments they have made about you. In fact, if you actually count, they may have said a hundred good things about you and only one negative comment. You suddenly feel that the relationship is doomed and that everything is over, failing to see all the warmth, joy, and fun you will have otherwise shared over the years. Another instance is if your boss gives you an overall glowing review but asks you to improve on a couple of aspects, and you come away convinced that you are a bad employee, and your job is on the chopping block.

### Overgeneralization

The example I provided when we dealt with the definition of distortions at the beginning of this chapter is one of overgeneralization. We use these to simplify the problem at hand or to make an excuse for our overreaction to things. For instance, you scold your child for always being "bad" or "naughty" for a few things they may have done out of curiosity. You may also be aware that as far as children go, your kid is not the worst of them and is usually obedient and well-disciplined. When you call them "all bad" or "a problem child," you are merely taking out your frustration on them. It is not really a reflection of who they are, but more a mirroring of your stress.

## Personalization

This is when we think that people are going out of their way to make life hard or miserable for us when the fact is that everyone is just doing the best they can for themselves. For instance, if somebody cuts you off in a traffic jam and gets ahead of you. You would most likely say, "What a jerk, taking advantage of me." Had you been anybody else, the person who got in front of you might have done the same. They did not do this to you; they were in a hurry, and they did what they could to get where they were going faster. The fact of life is that you become caught in many unfair things in life, not because you are bad, incompetent, or have failed, but because somebody had to accomplish something urgent, and they took a shortcut for themselves.

## The "Always Right"

Associated with the blame game, you must have encountered people who will never admit that they were wrong or that they made a mistake. They will always insist that they are right and that what they say or do is "always right." When you tell yourself that you can never be wrong, then that implicitly places the guilt or blame on others around you. Clearly, this is not an accurate picture of how things are because everyone makes mistakes. The inability to accept your share of the blame for things that do not turn out as unexpected is also a way of shirking responsibility.

### The "Should" or "Must"

These are individuals who can never say "no" and are perfectionists who always have to get things off their to-do lists. Their sentences will always be prefaced with "I should..." or "I must..." Their need to take care of everything by themselves will also mean that they will not delegate tasks to others, believing that if they do not do it, it won't come out perfect. If you suffer from this syndrome, you are setting yourself up for an early burnout.

The above are the sixteen cognitive distortions that generally prevent you from moving ahead of negativity. In the next section, I will tell you about my own personal struggle with these distortions.

## FROM PERSONAL EXPERIENCE

When I was younger, I experienced depression and anxiety frequently, but those weren't my biggest struggles. I had difficulty labeling my problem or identifying the underlying causes, which made me believe that there was something fundamentally wrong with me. At that time, I was unaware of cognitive distortions and how they can affect a person's thoughts and emotions. I did not realize that one could have multiple distortions at once, and this lack of knowledge made it difficult for me to understand and manage my mental health.

After reading about cognitive distortions, I finally felt a sense of clarity. However, it still took me several weeks to identify which distortion I was using in certain situations to ease my stress. In the next section, you will find a simple exercise whereby you can identify the cognitive distortion(s) that you are subject to. This will help you formulate a plan of action toward negating it in the future.

## IDENTIFYING YOUR COGNITIVE DISTORTION(S)

Even before we embrace the eight steps to conquer over-thinking, we need to have a fair idea of the cognitive distortions that we may be unconsciously using to reinforce the negativity that we harbor. One of the best tools that I have encountered for this is an online test prescribed by IDR Labs (*Cognitive Distortions Test*, n.d.). You can search for "*Cognitive Distortions Test*" in the references section of this book. It provides you with thirty-five questions, which you have to rank on a scale of "highly disagree" to "highly agree." You also have the option of marking "undecided" or "neutral," where you feel you aren't able to decide on a valid response. The questions are related to your emotive responses to common situations everyone faces. Based on your answers, this test will return not only a score of your cognitive distortion percentage but also a breakdown of the specific distortions you may tend to use more.

You can use the findings of this test as you embark on the eight steps we will be coming to next.

## TAKEAWAYS

> *I know it's hard to think positive when the negative is all around, but you have to try do not give up the fight before you have even begun it.*
>
> — CHRISTINA CASINO

Negative thinking can be a real block when it comes to manifesting our true potential. In the next chapter, we start on the eight steps to mental freedom, beginning with a flow and organization framework, re-energizing your brain, and avoiding the clutter that makes the brain spring to automatic thoughts.

# 3

# STEP 1—APPLYING ALLEN'S INPUT PROCESSING TECHNIQUE FOR ORGANIZED FLOW

You would imagine that step one to stop overthinking would be to change your thought patterns, right? However, in order for you to change or redirect your thoughts, you need to declutter and channel them first.

Think of a messy, dusty bookshelf with many torn, irrelevant, outdated books thrown in together with some amazing, life-changing ones you would love to read. For you to even identify the books that could have a tremendous impact on your life, you must first clean the shelf, decide which books to keep, which ones to dispose of, and probably even create a "will-decide-later" list of books to come back to. It is only once you organize this bookshelf that you can actually pick a book to take up and read.

The same goes for your mind. Managing your mind's flow and energy is the initial step that makes everything else easier. This will also provide a framework for the steps to come. Second, your brain spends a lot of energy in trying to create shortcuts to your subconscious problems (Roeling, 2017). When your ideas are more sorted, your brain can relax, knowing that there is no need to create shortcuts for these internal knots.

## WHY MENTAL ORGANIZATION AND DECLUTTERING MATTERS

There are a lot of advantages to creating mental shortcuts. These can be habit-forming tricks that will help you do mundane and routine tasks on autopilot without you having to think or spend too much energy on them. Hence, they will save a lot of time for you as well. However, there is a flip side to this. When you get into the habit of creating mental shortcuts for every task, this can also lead to lazy thinking patterns.

A HuffPost article (Gregoire, 2017) tells us why brain shortcuts are not everything they are cracked up to be. This was proven in an experiment conducted by psychologists at Duke University. They analyzed the efficacy of mental shortcuts based on participants who were given twenty dollars each and asked to choose between 1) keeping ten dollars or 2) flipping a coin to win or lose the entire twenty dollars. It was observed that most participants chose the first option, where they would retain ten dollars. In the second part of this experiment, the same participants were given twenty dollars again and a slightly reframed set of choices. They had to choose between: 1) losing ten dollars or 2) flipping a coin to win or lose the entire twenty dollars. Interestingly, this time most participants chose to flip for the twenty dollars.

If you look carefully at the two parts of this experiment, except for the phrasing of the language in the options, the exercise was exactly the same in both cases. However, as our brains are generally wired to "gain" rather than to "lose," most people preferred to go with option one in the first case, where they could "keep" ten dollars. They chose option two the second time because their brains latched on to "losing" the ten dollars, even though it would have allowed them to retain ten dollars exactly as before.

Cognitive shortcuts, unfortunately, seem to lead us back to poor decisions and distortions in our minds. Thus, it is in our best interest to get rid of them. This is where David Allen's Input Processing Technique comes in. Let us look at what this is and how adopting it can reap benefits for us.

## INPUT PROCESSING TECHNIQUE

The Input processing technique framed by David Allen (Lapaas, 2021) comprises five steps that allow you to remove your mental clutter, organize your thoughts, and then finally take action. The five steps, which we will be devoting some time to are: input, process, organize, review, and engage.

But before we go into the steps, let us quickly look at why this method, and specifically organizing your ideas, can be so beneficial.

- **Reduces stress:**

All of us have come across a situation when we must locate an important document we know we have placed in a drawer. The problem is that this drawer is overflowing with so many things, essential and nonessential, that just going through its contents and finding what we need is a pain. If your mind is cluttered to the point that you keep forgetting facts, events, or people, it leads to a lot of stress. Just as you feel anxious when you can't find your home or car keys, when you can't locate or recall information you once knew and need now, you feel angry, irritated, or depressed. Being organized can reduce this stress that we unnecessarily undergo.

- **Decluttering your emotions:**

Emotions are a tricky subject. People find it hard to disentangle the gamut of emotions that they experience. For instance, it is possible to be angry with a person you love a lot. You are happy with your work, and yet it may not be satisfying a part of you. People often think that emotions are all positive or all negative. But generally, the hardest part of them is that they are gray. When you learn to extricate what you actually feel from your emotional tangle, it can do wonders for your mental health.

- **A revolutionary way to rest and sleep:**

Remember they always told you that a person who is honest can sleep better? Well, I would rephrase that statement—someone who keeps their thoughts simple and better arranged will get more rest. You will not be kept awake by the endless possibilities in which things may go wrong. Instead, as you have already taken measures to give your thought-flow a certain order and method, you will find it easier to relax.

- **Increased endorphins:**

Yes, this may seem hard to believe because we are told that endorphins, or the "happy hormones," are chemicals released to produce pleasurable sensations or to block pain in your body. They are mostly associated with activities such as having sex or exercising. Science will also tell you that the more organized you are with your thoughts, your body will produce more endorphins (Flow Wall, 2016). This is because they are also produced where there is a good routine, which comes with an organized mind. The more you can train yourself to stick to a schedule, the more endorphins your body will release.

- **Increased productivity:**

If you are organized, you can get more done. Think of two people we shall call "A" and "B," respectively. A needs to get five things done. But not being very organized, they do not have the necessary paperwork or the materials required. They are also unclear about whom to contact to get certain parts of the tasks done. Thus, A uses half a day to undertake the research necessary and ends up completing three out of five tasks allotted to them. B, who also has five tasks to finish, already has the relevant files and contacts at hand. Thus, B is able to get through the tasks faster, without wasting too much time on research, and finishes all five tasks by the end of the day. This is pretty much the difference between an organized and disorganized mind. The former has all the prep work ready for when the time comes, while the latter is perpetually waiting till the moment arrives to start things.

- **Achieving goals:**

When you are organized mentally, you always have a plan of action. Having a blueprint of the entire process becomes second nature to you. If you want to do something, you have a Plan A and a backup Plan B in case A does not work out. When you are not organized, you are thinking on the go, which takes more time and energy. So, when Plan A does not materialize, that is when you start visualizing a Plan B. As a result, your mind is never fully focused on the larger picture. This makes achieving goals frustratingly harder.

- **Improves focus and attention:**

I would call this a mutual reinforcement. When you are organized, you are automatically more focused and attentive to details. Conversely, when you give more attention to the details, you become more organized. Like the chicken and egg conundrum, it would be difficult to tell which one is a product of the other. This is true even with relationships. If you are an attentive spouse, you will be cued into small details, such as your partner's expression and their verbal and nonverbal signals to understand that they are upset, long before they tell you. Asking them proactively why they are upset could help calm them down. Mental confusion can make you oblivious to your partner's upset.

- **Unlocks creativity:**

This might seem a little strange. After all, we have always grown up seeing the archetype of the "mad genius," the absent-minded professor, or the "eccentric artist," who have their heads up in the clouds, no matter how brilliant their work might be. Their work is usually always depicted as the product of a divine dream or a sudden artistic impulse. I am not discounting the fact that such individuals may exist. However, it is possible to have a certain "method to madness," as was so famously declared by Hamlet (The Idioms, n.d.). Most creatives and geniuses, no matter how preposterously unorganized they may seem on the outside, have a mental process in the organization of their work.

- **Clearing your mind:**

Being organized helps you clear and create space in your mind for tasks that really require it. If your mind is stuffed with thoughts like "get the grocery, renew the car insurance, clean the house, do the laundry, what's for dinner?" etc., you will not have the time or energy to focus on the new projects. You will feel mentally fatigued, trying to keep all the balls in the air. Instead, if you devise a time and space to tackle the routine in such a manner that they will not butt into the headspace needed to deal with more creative tasks. Organization will help you compartmentalize things better.

- **Managing time:**

"The conscious mind can only pay attention to about four things at once," is what Daniel Levitin, professor of behavioral neuroscience and psychology at McGill University, tells us (McGregor, 2014). The more organized you are, the better you can manage your time. As in the couple of examples we used above, you may not have to spend a lot of time on last-minute research if you already have the resources ready at hand. You will also train yourself in the art of getting things done quickly. You will have an established pattern of estimating timelines and getting either the smallest jobs done first, removing them from your to-do list, and then proceeding to the larger tasks, or vice versa. In short, you will devise the best possible methods to tackle the pile of personal, professional, and other errands on your plate in such a manner that you do not feel bogged down by them.

- **Puts an end to multitasking:**

Multitasking is often glorified in our world. It is supposed to be *the* way of functioning amidst the chaos that we face on an everyday basis. However, most psychologists and mental wellness professionals would agree with me when I say that multitasking is bad for you. The human mind is not biologically designed to multitask. It is simply a way that we have adapted over time to stay on track and complete work. However, multitasking at great speeds over long stretches of time is simply setting you up for mental and physical burnout. Daniel Levitin tells us how every time we multitask, our brain rewards us with a small dose of dopamine, the "happy hormone," which our bodies can get addicted to at the exclusion of even basic survival instincts for food or sex (McGregor, 2014).

The above are all the various ways in which organizations can help us put our minds on track. In the next section, we see how this can be done practically.

### The Five-Step Approach to Input Processing Technique

Decluttering your brain and organizing your goals, priorities, and flow is an essential step that paves the way for better brain energy and stopping automatic shortcuts. In this section, we will cover David Allen's Input Processing Technique (Lapaas, 2021), a five-step framework you can implement to achieve better organization and engage with your mind's flow state. So, let's discover the five steps to becoming mentally freer.

### 1. Declutter and externalize your mind's input:

Think of a computer that you use for work, entertainment, and finding information. Over time, you will find that its memory capacity reduces with every new document or video that you save to the system. Even if you do not download much, the files that are a part of daily net usage, such as cookies and other automatic downloads, will eventually slow down your system. Thus, it is essential to clean up the memory of the computer and also invest in an external memory device like a hard disk where you can store your favorite music, movies, and games without it affecting the efficiency of your device.

Your mind is not very different. Every day as you interact with the world, your brain processes new information such as sights, smells, tastes, linguistic patterns, feelings, emotions, and ideas. These sensory inputs can, at times, overwhelm your system. Your mind and body could feel "overloaded" by all the stimulation it receives from outside. If you do nothing about it, very soon, you will find yourself crumbling under the undue pressure that your system has to take. In order to declutter your mind, one of the best things that you can do is to externalize your mind's input. In other words, invest in a physical or digital journal so that you can clear up your brain for "thinking" rather than "remembering."

So, what does the above exactly entail? The following is a list that you can use to discover what suits your needs best. Below I've included a few items—from conventional sticky notes to online apps and platforms, which will help you to stay on top of your tasks:

- sticky notes
- calendars—virtual and physical
- a notepad

- a journal
- flash cards
- computer journals or diaries: You can use MS Word or any other word processing system on your computer.
- One Note: Online notes that you can create and save for whenever you may want to view them.
- Evernote: A notetaking and task management application
- Google Docs: Online word processor that gets saved and updated automatically on your Google Drive.
- Remember the Milk: The to-do app which will help you remember important things.
- Telepixie: Phone call support for reminders, wake-up calls, etc.
- Stickies: Tool to virtually stick important notes to your laptop's home screen.
- WiseMapping: Online mind mapping tool that will help you arrange the flow of your ideas.

You can try out the above to understand how each of them works and then choose an app or a platform that is secure, fast, and easy for you to use.

## 2. Process input within two minutes or prioritize something else:

The second step of Allen's technique is to process the information you have by asking yourself a few questions. If you answer "yes" to each one, finish the particular task. If you answer "no" at any point, stop doing what you are doing, and put it on a to-do list for later.

The questions you must ask are:

- **Is it actionable?** Suppose you receive an email from your colleague seeking additional information on a project you have handed over to them; you have to first ask yourself whether this task requires some action on your part. Since the answer here is "yes," ask yourself the question below.
- **Can I finish it in two minutes?** There's no point in procrastinating on something that can be completed in less than two minutes. So, for the case above, if you can send this file right away, do it. If you have to search for the file or are waiting on another person to fill in the relevant details, schedule this task for a little later on when you can do it in less than two minutes.

If the answer to the first question was "no," you can either save the communication for your reference or simply acknowledge the mail so that the sender knows you have received it.

After this comes the best part of this process, i.e., organizing.

### 3. Organize your input for processing and later returns:

After the previous step, you will have two categories of things to do: first, the ones you can tackle right away, and second, the ones you must schedule for a later time. There may also be actionable and nonactionable things that you have to sort and figure out where to put.

While organizing, the task, time, and context require special consideration. First, take up those actionable tasks for which you need to spend mental energy.

- Tasks like home improvement and lawn mowing come on the same priority list. However, tasks like responding to your child's request to go out with questionable friends or meeting a work deadline in an hour will come higher on the priority list. The latter is more urgent.
- Timely prioritization is a simple part of Step 3. A birthday has a date, so you can add it to your calendar. Also, a work deadline has a date and time, so ensure it is in your electronic planner or reminder app.

- Finally, context means prioritizing and organizing your to-do list by placing similar actions together to save time and energy. For example, allocating a time slot for all the phone calls you have to make is better than making them randomly throughout the day.

**4. Review what needs your attention frequently:**

A one-time use of the Input Processing Technique will not be sufficient to complete all the tasks. You will have to review what's pending and what's not from time to time and adjust your list accordingly. I would suggest a weekly review to ensure that you are on track with your list of things to do. Certain items may have to be moved to the high-priority section, and some others may have to be rescheduled. The main purpose of this review is to ensure that you are moving ahead (even if slower than you expected) and that there are no items on the list that you are putting aside.

**5. Engage with the flow:**

Being alive means that we go with the flow. Most things are repetitive, routine chores that we must take care of every so often. Making peace with this is half the battle won.

Following your action organization or to-do list is simple once everything is on paper (or on your device). Engaging with your new, organized life is much easier when you have easy access to your list of action points right in front of your eyes. Reviews will, of course, change your priorities as you discover more information on things. For now, just follow the two-minute engagement rule below.

## 6. Bonus—The Two-Minute Engagement Rule:

If you have five different tasks to be addressed in the day, it may not make sense for you to start with one, complete it, and then proceed to the next, especially when you have to show at least some progress on all of them. In such cases, David Allen's Two-Minute Engagement Rule would be very helpful. Whichever tasks can be completed in two minutes or less can be finished first. Then, divide the longer tasks into two minutes of productive bursts. So, tackle a particular task for two minutes, then move on to another on which you spend two minutes, etc. This will help you get started on all the tasks. However, you have to be mindful of the context of these tasks as well. Certain kinds of work require your full concentration, and frequently stopping and restarting them will be slower than if you were to complete them at a stretch (Perry, 2022).

## FROM PERSONAL EXPERIENCE

In his Ted Talk, Tim Urban talks of how he had to pull two all-nighters to complete a 90-page master's thesis because he started it just three days before the deadline. Despite his best intentions to work on it throughout the year, he was not able to start on it because of procrastination. He underwent a lot of stress in addition to the sleeplessness and made it just in time to drop it off just before the deadline. He also tells us that he did not get a great grade on the work (Williamson, 2019).

Urban's story is very relatable because it is something we all do. When we find that we have to do something unpleasant or something that might change our lives, we often put it off. I, too, did the same for a very long time in my life, until I figured out that it just delayed the inevitable and created prolonged and unnecessary stress along the way. I have realized that if I had not allowed procrastination and disorganization to get the best of me, I could have taken advantage of so many more opportunities that I instead let slip away and regret to this day.

The chart in the next section will help you implement a workflow to get things done.

## CHART THE INPUT PROCESSING TECHNIQUE IN YOUR LIFE NOW!

Use the chart provided below to bring more clarity into your life. It sets forth the stages of Allen's Input Processing Technique, right from selecting your planner to executing your tasks in an orderly fashion. You can modify the chart below as per your specific needs.

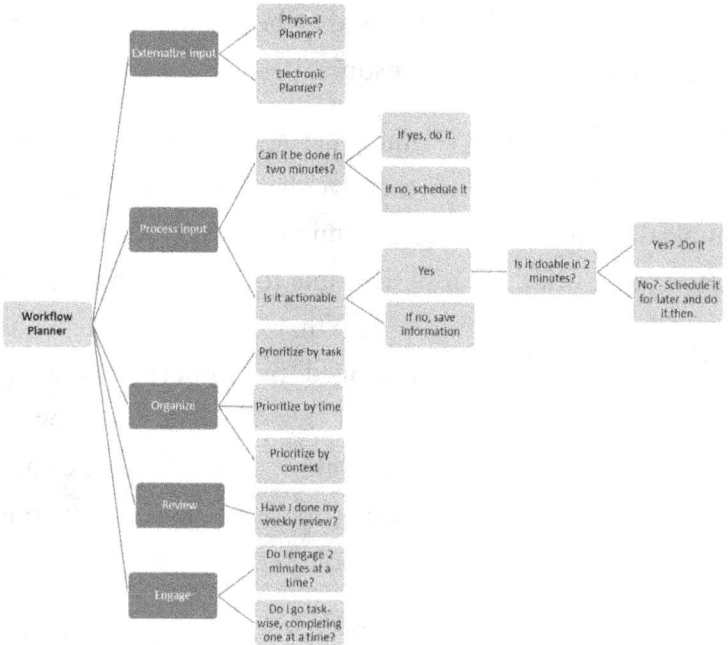

## TAKEAWAYS

> *For every minute spent in organizing, an hour is earned.*
>
> — BENJAMIN FRANKLIN

We looked at the five steps to using David Allen's method to organize your mindset and get things done. However, one of the biggest challenges you will face now is to identify your priorities. What would you do with extra hours? How much can you achieve toward your new mindset, goals, and priorities?

In the next chapter, let's discover how you can set priorities and goals for improved chances of success.

# 4

# STEP 2—PRIORITIZING YOUR LIFE AND THOUGHTS WITH EISENHOWER'S TECHNIQUE

David Allen's Input Processing Technique gave us five concrete steps to reduce the chaos inside our heads and keep it simple. However, there was a part of the exercise wherein we had to sort out tasks based on their priority, which could have been confusing. There may be at least a few of us scratching our heads, wondering how we go about this.

This chapter gives us an excellent tool to prioritize and decide in which order tasks, events, and other things should be handled. The method we employ here will also help in goal setting.

This method was developed based on President Dwight Eisenhower's iconic words, "I have two kinds of problems, the urgent and the important. The urgent aren't important, and the important are never urgent" (Team Asana,

2022). Eisenhower's Matrix uses this phenomenal concept to provide a guide to prioritization.

## EISENHOWER'S MATRIX

Eisenhower's Matrix relies on four keywords that you must remember. They are the 4Ds:

- Do
- Delay
- Delegate
- Delete

As you can see, all the four words above are related to task completion. The do-tasks are both urgent and important, while tasks to be deleted are neither important nor urgent. Tasks to be delegated are urgent but not as important, while those that can be delayed or scheduled are important but not very urgent.

| Importance | Urgency | | |
|---|---|---|---|
| More | More ——————————————→ Less | | |
| | **Do** | | **Delay (or Schedule)** |
| | Tasks with deadlines, targets, or consequences | | Important tasks contributing to personal growth but having no clear deadlines |
| | **Delegate** | | **Delete** |
| Less | Tasks that must be completed but do not require/can't be done with your skill sets | | Unnecessary tasks, distractions |

The following table will give you a better idea of the kind of tasks that fit into the four quadrants of Eisenhower's Matrix.

| **Do** | **Delay** |
|---|---|
| • A submission that has a deadline that is near. <br> • Your car broke down and has to be fixed. <br> • Your child is crying or needs help. | • A professional course that may improve your prospects. <br> • Planning for job change/ retirement. <br> • Servicing your car or other electrical equipment. |
| **Delegate** | **Delete** |
| • An urgent client request that does not need your personal handling. <br> • Booking flight or rooms for upcoming work trip. <br> • An email which can be sent by anyone in your team. | • Work meetings with no agenda. <br> • Checking your social media. <br> • Refurbishing your living room because you are bored of the same old. |

## *Quick Tips for Eisenhower's Matrix*

Apart from separating your tasks into the four quadrants the tips below can help you to prioritize:

- Color-code your tasks so that they visually represent the most urgent to least urgent. Choose your favorite colors, but I recommend the traffic light colors to start:

  - Tasks that are important and urgent = green
  - Tasks that are important but can wait = amber/ yellow
  - Tasks that are urgent but not important = blue
  - Tasks that are least urgent or important = red

- A cluttered matrix will be counterproductive. Do not allow more than ten tasks per quadrant because you will simply panic at the number of things to be done.
- Eliminate the tasks to be deleted before adding anything new to the other three quadrants. This will help you remove the nonessentials, like signing in and marking your attendance for work or updating your schedule, etc., before you sit down for the real tasks. There are also a bunch of things that make you "feel busy" without contributing in any real way to your personal or

professional progress. Get these tasks off your plate because they are hogging your time and keeping you from the things that you should be really doing.

- Use the Input Processing Technique to review and re-prioritize things weekly or to remove them from your priority list.

- Set your goals and priorities side-by-side. I'll be talking more about goal setting in a little while, but this can really help you plan out your life. Your short and long-term goals have to be worked into your list of priorities so that they will work together to improve your productivity. Ask yourself fundamental questions like: *What am I working toward?* and *What are my core ethics?* Both your Eisenhower's Matrix as well as your goals must answer these questions.

## SETTING GOALS IN LIFE

Goal setting is a vital part of planning your life. You can't afford to lose sight of your goals even as you deal with the nitty-gritty of life. In this section, we will analyze what it is, why it is important, and how it can be done. But let us look at two things that usually get in our way when we try to either do things or set goals for ourselves.

## Procrastination and Its Effects

Wise is the person who framed the proverb, "A stitch in time saves nine." Procrastination is the urge to set aside things. Sometimes it is not even a conscious decision. We think that we have all the time to get to certain tasks and then keep putting them off until they pile up into an unmanageable giant task, which you either can't possibly do or have to rush through (at the risk of your mental and physical health). Procrastination saps your energy because even when you do not attend to things, they remain at the back of your mind, bugging you and making it impossible for you to enjoy your leisure, hobbies, or entertainment. For instance, say you put your term paper on the back burner; every time you sit down to watch a TV show or just to hang out with your friends, thoughts of the paper you have not started haunt you.

## Negative Self-Talk

This is the other major setback that prevents us from completing our tasks and projects. Every time we think about doing something, a little voice in our head chimes in, *Oh, but this is beyond me. I can't do this. I am not smart enough, or disciplined enough, or I do not have the skills needed.* This negative inner voice keeps us from achieving our full and true potential.

Setting goals helps with both of the above. It will reduce your urge to procrastinate, as well as shut up the negative and self-sabotaging talk. So, let us look at how goal setting can be implemented.

### Step 1—The First Step and Dividing Work Into Manageable, Smaller Chunks

Taking that first step is often the vital key that most of us miss. Sometimes, we are so hung up on perfectionism that we are too scared to take that first step. But, even with the tiny mistakes, the thought that you are ready to commit to a task, or to take the plunge and give it your all, may be the push that you need to give yourself.

After you take the first baby step, there is no need for you to rush and do everything at once, either. Give yourself some time to get into the flow. For this, divide the work into small manageable chunks over the day, week, or month, depending upon its nature and how much time you have in total to complete it.

### Step 2—Mistakes Are Part of the Process

Often, it is our fear of making mistakes or of failing that holds us back. Instead, remember that nothing great was ever done by sitting back and worrying about it. So, actively give yourself the freedom to make mistakes and to learn from the journey. When you let go of the pressure to always be perfect, you give yourself more mental room to focus on the task.

### Step 3—Prepare for Obstacles and Take Breaks

Think of the possible obstacles that may come up while you're doing your work. This may take on the form of digital diversions, social calls, small errands that are urgent, etc. Make room for all of these. This means, do not overload your schedule with work-related items. Give some wiggle room for other emergencies which may creep in unannounced.

Similarly, give yourself a break after every hour or two. Remember, this is not a distraction or a favor you are doing to yourself, but rather much-needed time for you to recoup and restore yourself so that you can tackle work better. Rest is essential if you want to keep on top of your game.

### Step 4—Managing Your Environment

Pick a spot that is quiet, calm, and peaceful. Select music that will energize you and help you focus better. Tell friends and family that you will be busy during this specific time so that they do not unwittingly disturb you. Keep your phone physically as far away from you as possible because it is the biggest culprit in stealing time.

You can also think of a role model, emulating who will perhaps help you get motivated. When you feel that you are about to procrastinate, ask yourself what this person might do to keep going.

Now that we have looked at two specific setbacks that can deter you from achieving your goals and what you can do to overcome them, let us look at ways in which you can set goals.

## Methods to Set Goals

If you Google ways to achieve your goals, many methods will come up. However, there are two approaches to goal setting that stand out in their efficacy. These are simple to practice, easy to remember, and will guarantee you the results that you have always hoped for. These are SMART and GROW methods of attaining your targets. We will look at the merits of each of these next.

### SMART Goals

People in the management and commerce fields may be familiar with this acronym. This was first used by George Doran in his 1981 article "There's a S.M.A.R.T. Way to Write Management Goals and Objectives" in the *Management Review* (Pillans, 2021). Since then, people have adjusted the acronym so that it remains relevant to our needs today. SMART means the following:

- **S—Specific:** Every goal you set needs to be clear. For instance, "I need to get fit" is a very vague goal. Instead, saying something like "I need to go running every day" is a much more specific target.
- **M—Measurable:** Your goals need to have a value measurement so that you can ascertain whether you are on track. For example, "I need to lose at least 11 pounds to reach my ideal weight" is a measurable goal. The good thing about a quantity-based goal is that you can keep tracking your progress.
- **A—Assignable or Achievable:** When you set a goal, be clear as to what you will do in order to achieve it. In other words, you have to commit to it and hold yourself accountable for achieving or not achieving it. Keep repeating statements starting with "I will" so that you feel more in charge of your destiny.
- **R—Realistic:** If you are serious about achieving your goals, they have to be realistic. Saying things like, "I will change overnight and become fitter and disciplined," aren't realistic. When you aim for unrealistic targets, you are not only setting yourself up for failure but also for dejection, and you lose the will to try again.
- **T—Time related:** Every goal should have a time frame attached to it. Otherwise, you are merely going to fall back into the trap of procrastination.

"I will complete the diploma course in a year," as opposed to "I will complete that diploma course," will get you a better outcome.

## GROW Goals

Framed by business coaches Graham Alexander, Alan Fine, and Sir John Whitmore in the 1980s, the GROW model (Mind Tools, 2022) is another way in which you can go about trying to achieve your goals. GROW stands for the below:

- **G—Goal:** Think of a goal that is possible for you in a realistic timeframe. Imagine achieving this goal or get yourself as comfortable as possible visualizing this dream for yourself. The most important part of this step is to ensure that you are clear and certain about your goal—that it is something that you really want and see yourself getting.
- **R—Reality:** Here, you have to think of all the limiting factors responsible for keeping you away from your goal. These could include several things like financial obstacles, self-limiting thoughts, past failures, lack of appropriate skill sets, etc. Think of how you will bridge these gaps to step closer to the desired outcome.
- **O—Opportunities:** Now think of all the resources that you have at your disposal—

personal, professional, financial, etc. that you can use to move ahead and achieve your goal. You can also list potential opportunities that may be coming your way and that you plan to catch hold of. For instance, gaining access to the right contact at the right time can open doors for you more than if you were to do everything on your own.

- **W—Way forward:** This is possibly the hardest part of this model. W stands for the "way ahead" as equally as it does for your "Willpower." In other words, you have to constantly ask yourself whether you have it in you to stand and keep striving for your goal, whether you are willing to go on despite challenges, and whether the result will be worth all your hard efforts. Remember, attaining a goal is only possible when you are absolutely convinced that it is really what you want.

We have now seen how to prioritize tasks and enforce habit transformations through the Eisenhower Matrix. We also learned to set goals with one of the two models to establish a growth mindset gradually.

The cognitive distortions should lean heavily into your goals and priorities for changing your mindset from reactive to proactive. In addition, you can use Allen's framework, Eisenhower's Matrix, and the goal models to work through the upcoming steps. These steps will inspire goals and priorities in you if you have not already found inspiration via the first two steps of this book.

## FROM PERSONAL EXPERIENCE

I was intimidated when I decided to start working out regularly. I was a fitness enthusiast in my twenties, but the thought of going to the gym for an hour every day was overwhelming. But I also knew that I needed to make a change in my lifestyle, so I decided to take small steps and commit to just ten minutes of exercise every day.

I started by doing a few simple exercises at home, like push-ups and squats. At first, it was challenging, but I reminded myself that all I needed to do was ten minutes. Soon, ten minutes turned into fifteen, then twenty, then twenty-five, then thirty! I was proud of myself for committing to small steps and building momentum gradually.

By breaking down my larger goal into smaller, achievable ones, I was able to build my confidence and maintain my motivation. Over time, I began to enjoy working out and even started going to the gym regularly.

## PLOTTING GOALS AND GETTING THINGS DONE

Use or modify the tables below to come up with your own SMART/GROW method of setting goals. You can add rows where you feel there are more questions you may need to figure out on the way.

### SMART Worksheet

| | |
|---|---|
| **S:** Specific: Identify your goal; be as specific as you can about what and why you want it. | |
| **M:** Measurable: What is the quantitative part of your goal?<br>How often will you be able to measure progress? | |
| | |
| **A:** Assignable: How will you ensure your goal is attainable and relevant for you?<br>How will you hold yourself accountable? | |
| | |
| **R:** Realistic: Is your goal realistic? | |
| **T:** Time Related: What is the time frame you have to achieve this goal? | |

*Adapted from a worksheet from Positive Psychology (Sutton, 2020).*

## GROW Worksheet

| G: Goal | What is my goal? | |
|---|---|---|
| | What will my result look like? | |
| | Could there be any other results? | |
| | On a scale of 1–10, how sure am I that I can attain this goal? | |
| | How long will it take? | |
| | How will my goal help me? | |
| R: Reality | What is my current status on this goal? | |
| | What obstacles am I currently facing? | |
| | How can I turn these around? | |
| | What external strengths can I use? | |
| | What internal strengths can I use? | |
| O: Opportunities | What are the opportunities or resources that I can use to attain my goal? | |
| | Which opportunities seem the best at this point? | |
| | Which opportunities seem difficult right now? | |
| | Whom can I contact? | |
| W: Way forward | What is my first step? | |
| | When can I review my progress? | |
| | How will I hold myself accountable? | |
| | How do I celebrate my wins? | |

*Adapted from a worksheet from Positive Psychology (Sutton, 2020).*

*Note:* Use separate SMART/GROW sheets for different goals.

## Eisenhower's Matrix Worksheet

You can use the table below to set your Eisenhower's Matrix of tasks. Be sure to color-code them and review them weekly, though.

| Do | Delay |
|---|---|
| (Add tasks here that are urgent and important) | (Add tasks here that aren't urgent but important) |
| **Delegate** | **Delete** |
| (Add tasks here that aren't important but urgent) | (Add tasks here that are neither important, not urgent) |

## TAKEAWAYS

*The secret for getting ahead is getting started. The secret to getting started is to break your complex, overwhelming tasks into small, manageable tasks, and starting on the first one.*

— MARK TWAIN

In this chapter, we learned how to deal with two specific mindset challenges, namely procrastination and negative self-talk, and discussed three tools in all. Two of these tools help you set goals, and the third, in segregating your tasks by priority. We have seen how effective each of these can be.

In the next chapter, we look at another way in which we can counter our automatic negative thoughts, the CBT approach.

# 5

# STEP 3—USING CBT COGNITIVE RESTRUCTURING TO RESET THOUGHT PATTERNS

Cognitive Behavioral Therapy (CBT) is a long-trusted method to reset one's thought patterns. Its exercises require commitment, dedication, and endurance, but they get the job done because the techniques have been around for ages and have proven to be effective. Let's turn our attention to CBT thought retraining.

It is said that thoughts travel faster than light (Sivananda, 2021). So, how do you stop thoughts before they travel through your brain faster than lightning? Practice, and practice some more, is the only way to retrain your brain. This third step is realistic and practical. We have all heard the saying—"You can't teach an old dog new tricks." Changing your thoughts, habits, and beliefs can be a challenge for many. Let's go deeper and discover the truth about changing your mind.

## WHAT IS CBT? HOW CAN IT HELP?

It's no wonder you feel so mentally exhausted, especially once you discover how fast your thoughts travel. Imagine how many thoughts run through your mind every second. These thoughts trigger emotions, which in turn lead to your pattern of mental blocks, and you wonder, *how am I to feel inspired?* Let's use one of the most trusted frameworks for challenging and changing thoughts—CBT.

First, let's try to understand the connection between thoughts, feelings, behaviors, and circumstances. We respond to every situation or stimulus based on the core values we carry around. Our thoughts perceive this situation in a unique manner. Next, your emotions get involved, which triggers an action. CBT, developed by psychologist Aaron Beck, is grounded on the principle that what we do and how we feel are related to how we think. It is established that we can change the way we think. Thus, it is also possible to control our actions and emotions better via our thoughts (Ackerman, 2017a).

We are creatures of habit, and our automatic negative thoughts (ANTs) can disrupt our emotions and behaviors. This cycle will continue every time you find similar triggers or events, leading to the same loop of thoughts, resulting in the same negative emotions and behaviors. Fortunately for us, there is an intervention possible. You can interrupt the cycle, even with your thoughts running like jet aircraft.

Thoughts

Situation

Feelings

Actions

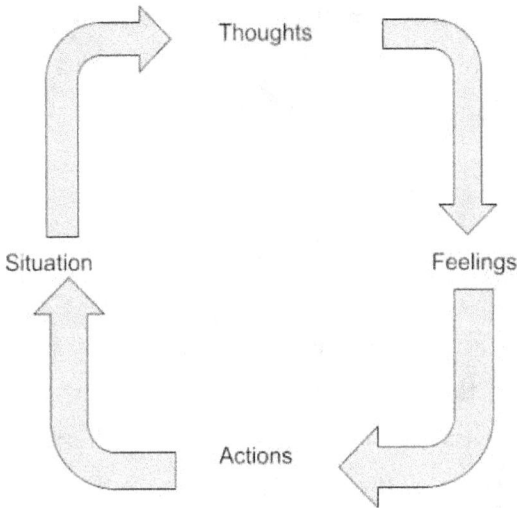

The brain receives signals about what's happening around you, typically through the senses. This is the "situation" you face.

Then, the core beliefs in your mind subconsciously nudge thought processes, which are faster than light. This part often relies on automatic habits, beliefs, and familiar situations.

Next, the emotional part of your brain starts firing in all directions, depending on whether you previously acted fearful, perceived the situation as a threat, or deemed it undesirable.

Finally, your behavior (or action) finds direction from the situation and your thoughts and emotions. Depending on how you reacted before, your body might fight, get scared, or you might say something you do not mean. Negative actions are often driven by your ANTs, and that is why without changing your thoughts, there is no changing your behavior.

### Interrupting the Cycle of Negativity With CBT

In the next couple of sections, we look at how we can change our thoughts and develop healthier and positive thinking patterns. You must start by understanding the process. However, incorporating them into your daily life will take some effort and practice. You can go step-by-step, as explained below, in getting yourself into the habit. Feel free to take your time to get comfortable with each step before progressing to the next step.

Ultimately, how you learn and practice the process is up to you. But remember that without working on all the steps below, it will be difficult to make any change or progress.

### Step 1—CBT Journal and Review

We already discussed the concept of cognitive distortions in Chapter 2. You might want to keep those notes handy before we proceed here. Next, we will learn to identify those distortions over the coming weeks and months by maintaining a "CBT Thoughts Journal."

The following aspects are what will go into your journal and what you will monitor. You can play around with how you want to visually present it, but each of your entries must capture all the four aspects provided below:

| Sl. No. | Date and time of event | Situation/ event | Emotion and its rating | Thought and its rating |
|---|---|---|---|---|
| 1. | | | | |
| 2. | | | | |
| 3. | | | | |
| 4. | | | | |
| 5. | | | | |

Every entry must start with a date on which the event or situation occurred.

Secondly, Give a brief description of the situation. What, where, who, how, why—answering the "wh" questions should sum up the main facts.

Now think of the main emotion you felt running through you. It is not just enough that you identify your emotion, you must also use a scale (1–5, or 1–10, etc.) to ascribe a value to the strength of your emotion. For example, "I was 3.5/5 angry with him right then."

In the last step, you must try to pin down the dominant thought that ran through your head at the time. Along with this, you also have to provide as accurate as possible value to the intensity of this thought. For example, "I believed 4/5 that he was lying to me."

Try to fill up the journal every week. The sooner you complete the journal after the situation, the more accurately you will be able to capture your thoughts and feelings.

Once you have started using the journal, you will also need to learn to analyze your thoughts, feelings, and actions for predictive patterns that you can trace. In other words, there may be many similar situations that awaken similar thoughts and feelings in you. When you learn to predict your reactions, then you are on your path to recovery and healing.

Review the four columns that you have filled in above. Now, use the following list of pointers to analyze your thought journal further.

- Review the event which caused you distress and ask yourself what you felt. Go over the intensity of emotion you felt as well as the subsequent thoughts. Ask yourself how much you believed in the thoughts that followed.
- Now ask yourself what "evidence" you had for believing as you did. Why did you draw a certain conclusion, and how justified was your conclusion?
- Is there any evidence against your conclusion? If you have been in this situation before, what happened then? Is there another way of contextualizing the situation?
- Could there be an alternative reason for what happened? Have you taken that reason into

consideration? Would you still be as upset if this was the real reason behind what happened?

Below is a worksheet (Classroom Mental Health, n.d. b) that will guide you in the predictive analysis process. Use the pointers above to complete it.

1. Recall and write about a stressful situation coming up shortly or one that keeps happening to you.

_____

_____

_____

_____

_____

2. Can you identify a couple of ANTs that accompanied the situation? Every ANT triggers an emotion in you, which you can note down in column two.

| Sl. No. | ANT | Emotion triggered |
|---------|-----|-------------------|
| 1.      |     |                   |
| 2.      |     |                   |
| 3.      |     |                   |
| 4.      |     |                   |
| 5.      |     |                   |

3. Try to think of coping thoughts that might help you feel better or less stressed about the situation.

i._____

ii._____

iii._____

iv._____

v._____

## Step 2—Restructuring and Reframing Your ANTs via Socratic Questioning

In this step you use CBT to restructure, replace, modify, or change your cognitive distortions around a certain incident so that you can feel better about it. CBT can help a person forge a more positive reaction toward people, places, and situations and reduce the stress and anxiety that you feel. The main benefit of using CBT in restructuring your thoughts is that you will no longer rely simply on your memory and feelings to explain an incident. Instead, you will learn to challenge and question some of your irrational feelings.

Socratic Questioning is one of the most widely accepted tools whereby you can do the above. Some questions you can ask yourself are

- Is my thought realistic?
- Am I assessing the situation based on my thoughts or feelings?
- Is there any evidence for what I am thinking?
- Could the evidence be wrong, or could I be misinterpreting it?
- Am I resorting to a black-and-white cognitive distortion?
- Is this a habitual thought or one supported by facts?

Think of something that you're currently obsessing about and is causing you to feel negative emotions. Start by asking whether what you feel is warranted, given the circumstances. Second, ask whether the stress you feel is driven by your emotions or your rational thoughts. Next, think of the evidence that supports this thought. Also, ask yourself if there might be another interpretation for the "evidence." Perhaps you are simply missing a link. Next, analyze your thoughts and consider if there are any cognitive distortions at play (see Chapter 2). Again, try to understand if your thought might belong more to a habitual pattern rather than one that is rational.

The diagrams below, adapted from Positive Psychology (Ackerman, 2018), will help you to restructure your cognitive distortion.

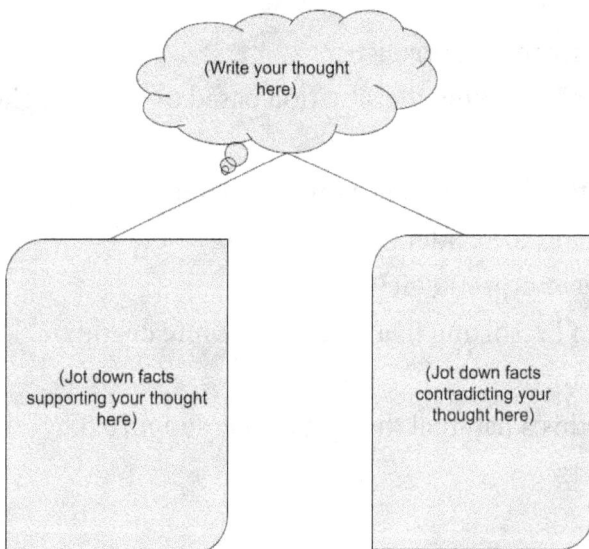

(Write your thought here)

(Jot down facts supporting your thought here)

(Jot down facts contradicting your thought here)

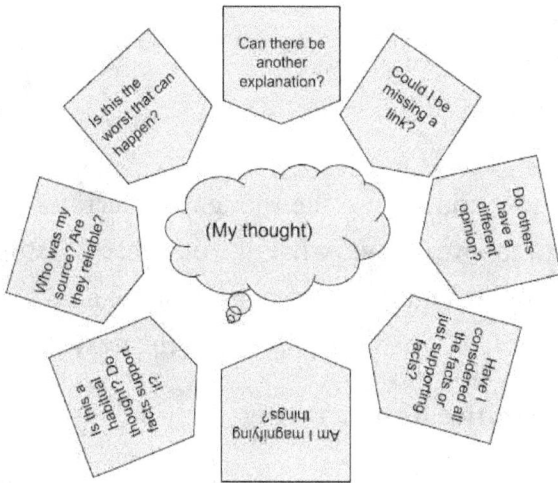

Can there be another explanation?

Could I be missing a link?

Is this the worst that can happen?

Who was my source? Are they reliable?

(My thought)

Do others have a different opinion?

Is this a habitual thought? Do facts support it?

Am I magnifying things?

Have I considered all the facts or just supporting facts?

(Your final verdict: Is your thought based on facts or feelings?

## Step 3—Finding Discrepancies

Now, based on your conclusion above, i.e., whether your thought is fact or emotion-based, this part of the exercise will aim to identify the long-term consequences of your thought. Think of the impact of your thought on things such as your

- future goals
- health

- financial goals
- friendships
- family relationships
- education or career goals

Think of how continuing the thought pattern will affect each of the above. Now, what if you were to stop the thought? How would that impact each of the above? Once you frame suitable answers, proceed to the next step.

**Step 4—Cognitive Restructuring**

Here, we try to combat the negative thoughts and convert them to something more positive, which will not eat up your mental energy and leave you feeling exhausted. Like the initial thought journal we maintained, you will record your thoughts again. But this time, try to find an alternative thought to replace your negative ones.

Columns one to five are what we already did in Step 1. You will have to spend a little time on the last two columns. For every ANT, come up with a best-case scenario first and then a realistic scenario. This will be your "adaptive response." In the last column, note the intensity of the negative thought after this exercise. Use the same scale you always use (1–5 or 1–10). Do you find the intensity of your negative thoughts is lesser now than in Step 1 of this chapter?

| Sl. No. | Situation | ANT | Emotion | Your response | A more adaptive response | Intensity of ANT |
|---------|-----------|-----|---------|---------------|--------------------------|------------------|
| 1. | | | | | | |
| 2. | | | | | | |
| 3. | | | | | | |

*Adapted from Positive Psychology (Ackerman, 2018).*

Let me help you a bit more with framing adaptive responses. The worksheet below will give you an idea of how to counter your ANT. In the left column below write down the worst possible outcome of a situation. On the right side, think of the best possible outcome. Now, in the middle column, think of a realistic possibility. I have given one example:

| Worst possible "what if" | Realistic "what if" | Best possible "what if" |
|--------------------------|---------------------|-------------------------|
| 1.  I fail the exam. | 1.  I get a decent grade in keeping with my level of preparation. | 1.  I get the highest grade. |

*Adapted from Positive Psychology (Ackerman, 2018).*

Now that we have tried the four steps to interrupt the cycle of negative thoughts, we will work on the core beliefs we carry with us.

## *Challenging Core Beliefs*

Core beliefs are the personal values that you assimilate over time with each experience you go through. Most people find changing or modifying this set of personal values difficult. But if you think some of your core values may be resulting in negative thoughts, feelings, and actions, then that is a sure indication that you may have to rethink them. This could be a taxing step, but one which will give you faster and surer results.

### Step 1—Facts or Opinions

This is the first stage of coping with your core beliefs. Frame a set of statements that you normally always think of. Next, try to sort these statements as "opinions" or "facts." Facts will have evidence or certain criteria to mark them as true. Whereas opinions will not have any facts backing them. They will be mostly based only on your emotional responses.

Here is an example with some model statements.

| Sl. No. | Statement | Fact | Opinion |
|---------|-----------|------|---------|
| 1. | I am not good-looking. | | ✓ |
| 2. | I let down my friend. | | ✓ |
| 3. | I shouted at my partner. | ✓ | |
| 4. | I am not very clever. | | ✓ |
| 5. | My BMI is on the higher side. | ✓ | |
| 6. | I am unlovable. | | ✓ |
| 7. | My mother said something hurtful. | ✓ | |
| 8. | I did something I regret now. | ✓ | |
| 9. | I am shorter than my friend. | ✓ | |
| 10. | My partner was intentionally cruel. | | ✓ |

*Adapted from Positive Psychology (Ackerman, 2018).*

As you can see above, the fact statements are based on something that happened. The opinion statements are just general conclusions you have drawn.

## Step 2—ABC Functional Analysis

At this stage, you identify certain events or incidents you underwent in the past. Recall your response at the time. In the last column, try to understand why the response was a negative one and what consequences (physical, mental, emotional, financial, professional, personal, etc.) it can have for you.

| Antecedents (What was the situation you faced?) | Behavior (What was your response? —action or words.) | Consequences (What was the potential negative outcomes of my response?) |
| --- | --- | --- |
| There was a lot of work to complete. I was under a lot of stress. | I shouted at my coworker. | I could be passed up for a promotion because the committee will think I am incapable of handling pressure. |

*Adapted from Positive Psychology (Ackerman, 2018).*

## Step 3—Converting Behavioral Tests to Core Values Worksheet

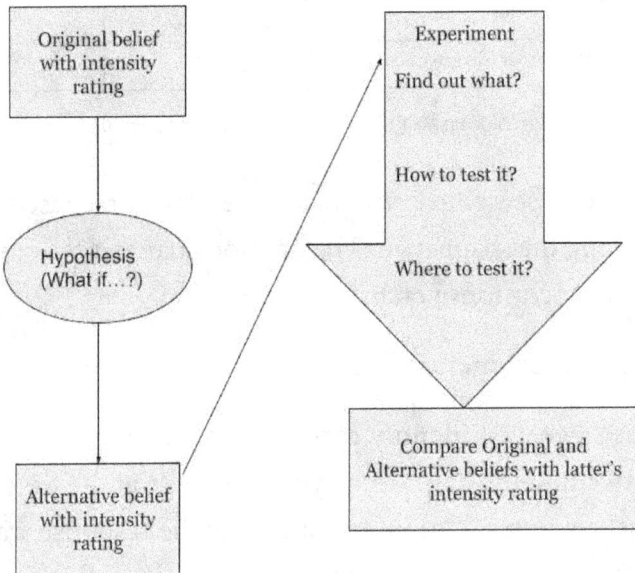

*Adapted from Positive Psychology (Ackerman, 2018).*

The five stages of this step are as below:

1. Think of one of your core values that often leads to ANTs.
2. Think of a hypothesis, i.e., what if you used another value in place of the original one?
3. Think of this alternative belief and whether it serves your purpose.
4. How can you put this alternative belief to the test? Where can you try it on yourself, and what outcomes are desirable?
5. After testing the alternative belief to be valid and true, compare the intensity of belief you have in the two thoughts. Accept the one you can believe more.

**Step 4—Logging Positive Beliefs**

Once you have found a new belief or value to replace your old one, this last step is all about enforcing this in your life. In the table below, record your old and new beliefs. Now list the facts that support your new belief. This method will help you dislodge the old belief further from your mind, with all the evidence in support of the new belief.

| Old belief: | New belief: |
|---|---|
| **Facts supporting new belief:** | |
| 1. | |
| 2. | |
| 3. | |
| 4. | |
| 5. | |

*Adapted from Positive Psychology (Ackerman, 2018).*

With this, we come to the end of using CBT to question, dislodge, and displace old beliefs leading to ANTs and breaking the cycle of negativity.

## FROM PERSONAL EXPERIENCE

One morning, I woke up feeling irritable and groggy. I noticed that my mind kept dwelling on negative thoughts. *I do not want to go to work today. I have so much to do, and there's no way I can make my deadline.* Infuriating thoughts such as these kept returning, no matter what I did.

The thoughts continued, and I felt my mood becoming even more negative. I was even irritable with my family. I decided to take a walk and get some fresh air. As I walked, I made a conscious decision to stop thinking negatively and focusing on the things that were stressing me out. I began to consciously think about the things I was looking forward to, like the joy I feel when supporting colleagues and clients. Suddenly, I started feeling much better. I could feel my mind and body relaxing. By the time I returned home, I felt more energized and positive and able to tackle the tasks ahead.

## SOME COPING THOUGHTS

This is an exercise that you can easily practice. It draws on everything we have discussed thus far. In a table like the one below, list all your most common ANTs on the left side. On the right side, note down a corresponding realistic but positive thought. Use this table every time you have an ANT to consciously convert it into a coping strategy.

| ANT | Coping thought |
|---|---|
| I am ugly. | I may not become a model, but I am beautiful. |
| I'll never do well at anything. | There are things I am good at and can do well. |
| I'll fail my exam. | I may not get the highest grade, but with effort, I can get a decent score. |
| I'll never get into a good college. | I'll put in more effort, so I can make it to a good college or find a job I am proud of. |
| My parents do not understand me. | Let me try talking to parents and explaining my side of the story. |

You are free to use the examples above and add to them as you see fit. Ultimately, your table of coping thoughts should resonate with your specific problems and help you with your anxieties.

## TAKEAWAYS

> *While you were overthinking, you missed every-thing worth feeling.*
>
> — NITYA PRAKASH

It's true, you will miss many wonderful feelings over-thinking and spending your energy on negative thoughts or opinion-based beliefs. Do not miss out on life and all that is beautiful. Instead, restructure what you think, believe, and feel. Then, you can discover how feeling good from within can do wonders in stopping your over-thinking and rumination.

In the next chapter, we look at a tool that will help you reconstruct your emotional makeup.

# 6

# STEP 4—RATIONAL EMOTIVE THERAPY FOR EMOTIONAL RECONSTRUCTION

A big part of changing your cognitive distortions and your ANTs into positive thinking has to do with putting reasons back into your emotional responses. Rationalizing emotions can be tough, but there's no need to overcomplicate the process. This chapter will guide you through the fourth step of the journey, which looks at targeting the emotional part of your habits.

Emotions can be either rational or irrational (McKay & McKay, 2019). Distinguishing rational from irrational emotions is a way to gain self-control over your feelings that trigger behaviors like overthinking, rumination, and procrastination. So, let's discover what rational and irrational emotions are and which of the feelings you can control, applying the laws of logic.

## EMOTIONS

What are emotions? You likely thought *they were our feelings.* Emotions are our feelings, but they also go beyond the everyday feelings of rage, boredom, happiness, sadness, jealousy, etc. Emotions can be a vital part of who we are. People tend to elevate thoughts over emotions. In fact, we are often taught that they form a pair of binaries, such as thoughts vs. emotions. The connotation is that thoughts are rational, based on facts, and somehow superior to emotions, which are based on our feelings and how we respond to situations.

The fact of the matter is that emotions are a very important part of who we are, and they are just as necessary as our thoughts. Let us see what the functions of emotions are, or rather what purpose they serve.

- **Emotions Recognize a Value:**

When someone whom you were very close to dies, do you not feel sad? Sometimes the sadness may turn to anger. For instance, "Why did that person have to die?" We recognize both these emotions as quite natural. However, if you hear of a random stranger's or a passing acquaintance's death, you may feel pity, but it does not move you in the same manner. This is also justified—why would you mourn their death as much as that of a dear friend or family member's?

When you are greatly wronged, do not you feel angry? If the person who wronged you turns out to be a good friend, you are even more angry. *How dare this person whom I've always treated with respect, kindness, and sincerity do this to me?* Something along these lines would be your response. This, too, is natural.

But suppose you feel no emotion whatsoever at the passing of a close relative or no indignation at being cheated on; is that normal? To be human is to feel, and certain situations warrant certain emotional reactions. Otherwise, most people would say you are "cold-blooded," "mentally unstable," or even downright "scary." Thus, emotions recognize a certain value of what other people, places, or objects mean to you. Only a person for whom nothing in life held any meaning would be incapable of emotions.

- **Emotions drive actions:**

You were humiliated by a teacher or a student in class who told you that you are dumb and that you'd never amount to much in life. You are extremely angry because you know you aren't dumb, and you are fired up to prove the point. So, you devote more hours to studying and finally end up being top of the class. Does this sound familiar? Emotions are the agents that push us to take action.

Even negative emotions like anger, jealousy, and fear can be channeled to great heights of productivity. You must have heard of survival stories, where people are trapped in unfamiliar terrains like jungles or caves and come out alive after months. Most of these people will tell you that their intense fear kept them alive. They are so sensitive to danger that they instinctively use their fear to protect themselves from wild animals or the elements.

- **Emotions can be strategic:**

It is true that we often tend to look at emotions as something that is self-sabotaging. People are often told to be less emotional and more rational to increase their chances of success in life. Though, in theory, it does sound rather great, it is very hard to put into practice. Not all emotions take you away from the path. As in the examples I've used above, anger, love, jealousy, and fear can be channeled to achieve great and terrible things.

Let me give you examples of numerous crimes of passion driven by love and jealousy rather than by hate. Most of the culprits, when caught, will admit that they murdered out of their love for the person. Though we may find this unfathomable, and dismiss their sentiment as irrational, most of these murderers are anything but. In fact, the cold, calculated precision with which they plan and kill their victims proves that emotions can indeed be very strategic. I have used a dark example here, but my argument still stands valid.

- **Emotions create meaning:**

Why are we attracted to certain people and not others? Why do we feel certain objects to be of more value than others? Why do some places evoke feelings of awe and wonder in us? The reason is that emotions are a vital tool that helps us provide context and create meanings for us. Without emotions, we would be like robots, having only a single program running all its analytic functions. But the human brain is a complex machine that takes into account past experiences, and feelings, in the meanings we create for ourselves. This is what distinguishes one person from another. This is also why we are drawn to other people in a web of friendship, familial, and romantic ties, whereas some other people make absolutely no impact on our psyche. Emotions also give you a purpose in life. A mother trains herself to survive because she knows that her survival is essential for the survival of her children.

- **Emotions can be trained:**

You may have perhaps thought that only thoughts can be organized. However, emotions, too, can be trained. We can train ourselves to see the positives in situations over time and gradually become more optimistic in our outlooks. The reverse is also possible, as we have seen.

Give yourself over to every negative emotion that comes along, and gradually bitterness, anger, or pessimism can become your dominant nature. This is also perhaps why wise people ask us to "pick our battles carefully." For instance, not all anger is bad, as long as we know how to use it for positive outcomes for ourselves.

- **Correct emotional allocation will lead to a healthy mindset:**

When we learn to counter situations with the right emotional response, it can be a healthy outlet for our mind. By this, I do not mean that there should only be one emotional response for all the people who might face the same situation. The right emotional response for bringing the best outcomes will help you overcome obstacles, move on, and find personal success. In short, you need to identify the emotional release that will help you find closure or help as a catalyst for change in your life. Rational emotions will also help you cope with failure and to accept it as a part of life and not as a part of you.

*Rational and Irrational Emotions*

Since we have established that we need emotions to survive and just be human, we need to identify those emotions that will propel us to take smart action and encourage us to do the best possible for ourselves. These actions are what we term "rational emotions." In this section, we will look at definite methods to boost our rational emotions.

One of the easiest tests to differentiate between rational and irrational emotions is to ask yourself the following questions:

- *Does the way I feel help or hinder my progress?* If it helps you, then it is rational.
- *Are my feelings logical, realistic, or based on the truth?* If you answer "yes" to any of these, again, your emotions are rational.

Now, let us look at the differences between rational and irrational thoughts:

| Rational thoughts | Irrational thoughts |
|---|---|
| Are driven by logic and reasoning | Are driven by neither logic nor reasoning |
| They are based on valid, well-thought-out beliefs | They are based on ill-perceived beliefs and thoughts |
| Cause rational or mature emotions | Cause irrational, illogical, or hasty emotions |
| Cause rational or mature actions | Cause irrational, immature, and illogical actions |
| Examples: Your friend did not return the book you lent them, and you are angry with them. Somebody complimented you on your appearance, and you are happy. | Examples: Your manager promoted somebody else over you, instead of talking to your manager, you shout at your coworker. Your partner is still occasionally in touch with their ex. You pretend you are fine with this but secretly feel insecure and angry with your partner. |

We have looked at what rational and irrational emotions mean. We will now look at the tool that will help you formulate more rational emotions in you.

## RATIONAL EMOTIVE THERAPY (RET)

RET is the answer to how you can discover new ways to be emotional without negatively impacting your progress, procrastinating, or overthinking. The main step of RET is to recognize the negative thoughts and feelings that hinder your choices and life. Let's learn more about it.

RET (Raypole, 2018), introduced by Albert Ellis in the 1950s, is a method that will help you identify your negative thoughts that could be causing emotional problems. At this point, you may ask how RET is different from CBT. They are similar processes. However, RET focuses more on the emotions behind the ANTs, while CBT focuses on the negative thoughts themselves. RET also gives a lot more emphasis on self-acceptance. RET has been found to be particularly effective among those suffering from depression, anxiety, phobias, procrastination, and a host of other psychological issues.

RET has three main targets, which are:

1. Increasing your problem-solving skills (which we will get to shortly).
2. Using cognitive restructuring (Covered in the last chapter and which helps you recognize the emotions and situations that require change or rationalization).

3. Applying coping mechanisms (which you will encounter in the next chapter).

RET has three ABCs to it, which make up its core strategies:

1. **A:** Learning to manage the **A**ctivating event, or the event that causes you stress, anger, or the negative emotion.
2. **B:** Changing your irrational **B**eliefs, which helps you become a more balanced individual.
3. **C:** Coping with the emotional **C**onsequences of irrational thoughts.

Next, we will look at how problem-solving techniques can be implemented to solve some of the ill effects of irrational thoughts.

## USING PROBLEM-SOLVING TO NEGATE THE CONSEQUENCES OF IRRATIONAL FEELINGS

To begin with, there are two incredible RET exercises that utilize exposure-style therapy, allowing you to envision the worst-case scenario and better prepare for it. In most cases, your preparation would be for a far worse case than the actual situation, easing the emotional consequences of facing it. It's an excellent exercise to use before exams or other stressful situations.

*Imagine the Worst Exercise*

Catastrophizing about the worst that can happen is a distortion that is more common than you would imagine. This exercise will help you realize that the worst eventuality is unrealistic, and the odds of it happening are minimal. The time and energy you spend agonizing over it could probably be more draining than if you were to actually deal with it.

The following exercise, adapted from Positive Psychology (Ackerman, 2020), may cause an increase in anxiety initially. However, in the long term, it will help you organize your emotional responses in a more positive frame.

1. Imagine an upcoming situation or event that is stressing you. Now think of the very worst outcome that this could lead to. Imagine all the minute details to make it as authentic as possible. For instance, you can't submit that all-important report you have been working on for weeks, and your boss calls you over into their office. What are the worst things they could say to you? Would they fire you? How would this make you feel?

2. Now, think from your perspective. How does the situation make you feel? Would you still feel bad the next day? What about in a week's time—will the event still seem as important? In a month, will you still be as unhappy over the same thing?

3. If this situation were to play out, what are the things you could change or control to make it less intimidating?

Now that you have done this exercise, move on to the one below (Ackerman, 2020).

***Blowing Things Out of Proportion Exercise***

1. Imagine the same thought that is causing you stress, anxiety, and sleeplessness.
2. Blow this situation out of proportion so that it becomes ridiculous or wildly impossible. Make it as laughable as possible in your head.
3. Laughing at your fears can make them less intimidating. You will feel more in control of them and, consequently, less insecure about yourself.

In the example above, try to visualize yourself stumbling and falling down as your boss is telling you off. You try to stand up, holding a chair for support, which slips from your hands, and you fall down again. Think of your boss' shock and outrage as you stand up only to fall down yet again. You are called in front of the disciplinary committee, where you keep falling, but now you are laughing, and so are some members of the committee. This ludicrous situation will help you cope better with the crippling fear you have been feeling regarding this situation.

## *Disputing Irrational Feelings Quiz*

There is one more problem-solving technique that will help you deal better with irrational thoughts and emotions. The following exercise, also adapted from Positive Psychology (Ackerman, 2020), will help you curb some of those self-sabotaging, irrational beliefs that hamper your growth in personal and professional situations. As you answer each question below, spend 10 to 15 minutes thinking about and writing your responses.

1. Describe one self-defeating thought you would like to get rid of.

_____

_____

_____

_____

2. Is there any evidence to prove this thought?

_____

_____

_____

_____

3. Can you find facts to contradict this thought?

_____

_____

_____

_____

4. What do people you trust think about your belief? Do they agree or disagree with you?

_____

_____

_____

_____

5. What could be the worst possible outcome of continuing to believe what you do?

_____

_____

_____

_____

6. Describe this in detail—what will happen, how would you feel, who will witness the situation, where will it happen, etc.

———————————————————

———————————————————

———————————————————

———————————————————

7. What positive things could happen, even if this worst-case scenario happens? Think hard and try to think of at least three positive impacts.

———————————————————

———————————————————

———————————————————

———————————————————

8. What do you now feel about your initial thought? Does it feel worthwhile holding onto it?

_____

_____

_____

_____

9. How are you going to break the cycle of this negative thought?

_____

_____

_____

_____

10. How are you going to implement disrupting this negative thought daily?

_____

_____

_____

_____

## HOW TO USE THE RET PRINCIPLES

When you use RET principles to change your emotions to a more logical approach, you will feel a lot more emotionally liberated. RET inspires steps that you can follow before deciding or reacting to a situation.

You can also use the steps below to slowly shift your thoughts and interrupt the automatic emotional process. You can change your feelings and beliefs to a more rational tempo.

1. **Pause to assess:** When in doubt, do not rush thoughts, decisions, or choices. Take it slow and always think of its implications for you in the short and long term. If you are still unsure, give it some time, or come back to it later for contemplation.

2. **Do not go by your gut instinct:** Gut instincts can be a great pointer toward a general direction, but they aren't always right. Therefore, even if you feel something is not right, take some time and think of it from all angles before you make a final call.

3. **Frame it in writing:** There is a reason writing has been called "therapeutic." Putting things in writing always gives you a framework or a blueprint. Thus, it will also help you focus on the facts better.

4. **Narrow down your options:** Elimination is a great way of arriving at your final choice. Proceed from what you definitely do not want and work your way to the things that you may probably want. This will help you narrow down your choices so that you do not grapple with the confusion of too many things to choose from.

5. **Take the majority opinion:** Ask people for their opinions. I am not saying that you must blindly accept their suggestions. But listening to many opinions will help you better clarify your feelings and thoughts on the problem at hand.

6. **Sleep on it:** If you want to avoid burnout, one of the best methods to do so is to sleep on it. Even experts claim that when you sleep, your brain synthesizes patterns and new neural pathways (Antonio, 2016). When you wake up, your mind is refreshed enough to find a solution.

The process above helps to make better decisions and feel differently by interrupting the automatic process, but do not expect it to go smoothly the first time. It requires practice and commitment. Meanwhile, it also boosts your problem-solving skills, allowing you to move irrational thoughts and feelings to a logical conclusion slowly.

Using the above steps, I know that I have learned to deal with my emotions far better. In fact, let me tell you of an incident and how I came to terms with it.

## FROM PERSONAL EXPERIENCE

Like most people, I've had relationships with people who weren't right for me. There is one in particular that I truly regret. This man seemed to really love me and wanted us to get married and plan a future together. I loved him, but not the way I felt a wife ought to love her husband. He was an extremely nice guy, and I thought that my love for him would grow, so I said nothing and went along with planning a future with him. After a couple of years, I realized that I couldn't continue and that my feelings hadn't grown for him. He was deeply hurt and accused me of emotionally manipulating him by hiding my true feelings and disregarding him. Although it was hard, and I wished things had been different, I was relieved to be free.

Looking back, I knew he was wrong for me a long time before he caught on. I should simply have admitted it to myself and to him. Instead, I wasted both my and his time and energy in a relationship that would never have worked.

## BEYOND THE COMFORT ZONE

Comfort zone → Fear zone → Learning zone → Growth zone

There are two "zones" that one should be a little wary of in life—the comfort zone and the fear zone. The comfort zone is a trap that entices you with security, but you often find yourself bored and undervalued there. The next is the fear zone, in which the fear of the unknown keeps you trapped in known situations, even though they may not be ideal for you. In both these stages, you do not grow as a person because you do not move ahead of your current situation. A combination of comfort and fear makes us stay in toxic relationships or bad work environments simply because our minds can't think beyond them.

Jumping into the learning zone will help you keep both comfort and fear at bay. On the one hand, there will be the excitement of gaining new knowledge, and on the other, the constant process of learning will not give you time to wallow in fear or anxiety. When you stay in the learning stage for a while, that is when you will reach the growth zone. The minute you stop learning, you will move back into the comfort and/or fear zones.

Take a minute now and think of five things that make you afraid. Now record them, along with reasons you fear learning or doing them.

_____

_____

_____

_____

Now try to think of how you can overcome these fears through learning and growth, the two zones that are so vital to change your mindset.

_____

_____

_____

_____

## TAKEAWAYS

> *What worries you, masters you.*

— JOHN LOCKE

You can't decide on emotions or find solutions to stop overthinking, procrastination, or ruminating without mastering your emotional process. The six steps will get you there, but you will also need carefully designed training to develop coping mechanisms. In the next chapter, that is exactly what we will talk about.

# 7

# STEP 5—AUTOGENIC TRAINING TO MAKE ON-THE-SPOT DECISIONS

It's important to realize how vital emotional stability is to your progress in this journey. The more stable your emotions become, the more control you will have over your thoughts, decisions, beliefs, and cognitive restructuring.

Emotional intelligence allows you to make effective, on-the-spot, logical decisions (Goleman, 2019). So, how can you build emotional intelligence? How can you create a stable emotional state on which your decisions are based to prevent overthinking and procrastination? In the fifth step of your journey, these are some of the questions that will be answered here.

## EMOTIONAL INTELLIGENCE

The ability to understand, interpret, control, and demonstrate emotions appropriately in your interactions with people is called emotional intelligence (Cherry, 2022b). Emotional intelligence would include things like being empathetic to others' feelings, being confident about your decisions, being able to let go of mistakes, taking responsibility for your mistakes, having an idea of personal thoughts and values, etc.

Emotional intelligence requires the following:

- **Identifying emotions:** What am I feeling?
- **Comprehending emotions:** Why am I feeling this way?
- **Negotiating emotions:** Is there a better way to feel under the circumstances?
- **Managing emotions:** How can I be better prepared for things emotionally?

Emotional intelligence is an extremely crucial tool in self-analysis because it will help you in the following ways:

- You will be able to think well before doing something on an impulse.
- It will build your capacity for self-awareness and knowing yourself better.

- You will become more empathetic, i.e., able to put yourself in another person's shoes and see things from their perspective.

Let us now explore some quick CBT methods (Psychology Compass, 2018) to improve emotional intelligence when facing decisions, getting started on a task, or putting an end to ruminating thoughts.

- **Use integral emotions:**

All the feelings associated with making a decision—the uncertainty, anxiety, excitement, etc. are integral emotions of the process. Instead of pushing them away, deliberately engage with them and find out what you would be most comfortable with. You need to be able to control and channel these emotions to help you make the decision. Secondly, use how your body responds to your emotional cues to select an alternative that is most in keeping with your personality.

- **Use the time-delay strategy:**

Remember how we talked about not rushing to make decisions—maybe even sleeping on them? Time can often bring a new perspective on the situation. When you use time to delay a decision, you can also distance yourself from the immediacy of your emotional response. This will automatically make your decisions more rational.

- **Approach incidental emotions with caution:**

Incidental emotions are those feelings surrounding the situation but not directly linked to it. Assume you are already in a good mood on a day when someone asks you for a loan. Your good mood impedes your decision-making, and you end up giving them the money, though you know that this person is not very reliable and has a history of not keeping their word. You must always rely more on integral, rather than incidental, emotions and learn to separate the two.

- **Avoid accidental emotions:**

These are emotions wrongly attributed to the situation at hand, thus, distorting your perception and decisions. For instance, you had a bad relationship a little while ago and are suffering from trust issues. You meet somebody who is very unlike your previous partner and possibly even a good match for you. But because your ex treated you badly, you expect the same from this new person. Thus, you are not able to separate your past experience from your present one.

- **Use the 4 As of stress management** (Sparks, 2019):

| Avoid | Alter |
|---|---|
| Avoid negative things, people, and situations that you can't change or do anything about. Learn to say "no" where you have to draw boundaries. | Alter your responses to situations and people so that you can see them in a different, more positive light. Manage time better or state your differences of opinion respectfully with people. |
| **Accept** | **Adapt** |
| Accept that certain things are just the way they are. Worrying will not do you any good. Learn from your mistakes and forgive yourself and others wherever possible. | Look at the big picture or from a different perspective. Reframe the problems so that you can deal with them better. |

We looked at some temporary situations in dealing with improving your emotional responses to situations. However, real and lasting change can only come from autogenic training. In the next section, we see what this means.

## AUTOGENIC TRAINING

Autogenic (which means "self-generating") training or therapy was introduced by Johannes Heinrich Schultz in the 1920s as a way of coping with the physical effects of stress (Lindberg, 2019). Practitioners of this method use different relaxation techniques for the body and mind. Even today, autogenic training is used with CBT to combat negative thinking and stress.

Autogenic training has been proven to be effective in various disorders such as anxiety, depression, social anxiety disorder (SAD), general anxiety disorder (GAD), and sleep disorders. It works by lowering blood pressure, slowing down breathing, and grounding the body in an aura of wellness.

Though it can be eventually practiced individually at home, it is always best to start it as a guided session under an expert. They will teach you the six methods to attaining autogenic wellness for your body and mind. The training will include breathing exercises, verbal cues, repetition, and focus on certain body parts.

Let us look at the six techniques (*Autogenic Training*, 2016) which are a part of autogenic training.

1. **Inducing heaviness:** This step consists of verbal cues to focus on a certain body part and feel a heaviness in it.
2. **Inducing warmth:** Here, we train our mind to feel warmth in a particular body part and feel it spreading to the rest of the body.
3. **Heart Practice:** Here, we use our heartbeats as our focal point of reference to channel our attention.
4. **Breathing Practice:** In this step, we use breathing as a medium to feel calmer and more in control of our senses and thoughts.

5. **Abdominal practice:** We use verbal cues to specifically focus attention on the gut region and its feelings.

6. **Head Practice:** These are verbal cues used to feel and maintain a sense of coolness in your forehead area.

Verbal cues sound like—"I am calm," "My breathing is relaxed and natural," "My arms feel a heaviness," or "My head feels light, cool, and relaxed." Each of these statements is often repeated a set number of times as per the therapist's recommendation.

The aim of the entire process is to make the trainee feel relaxed, calm, and more self-reflexive. After a certain duration of guidance-led training, the trainee can resume the practice on their own, at home.

Here is a quick way to conduct a home session (Lindberg, 2019) for yourself:

1. **Build the right atmosphere:** Start by setting up the area where you plan to do your training session. It must be a cool, clean, well-ventilated, and silent place where you feel at ease. You can either sit or stand as you practice the therapy.

2. **Focus on your breathing:** Start by inhaling and exhaling slowly. Remember to expand your chest when you draw in air and to relax when you breathe out. Whenever you find your mind

wandering, as it will in the beginning, bring it back gently to your breathing.

3. **Bring your attention to various parts of your body:** Now start with any body part and repeat a statement such as, "My right arm feels heavy. I am calm." Now, repeat the same with other body parts, but keep reminding yourself that you are calm.

4. **Focus on your heartbeat:** Tell yourself, *my heartbeat is regular, and I am calm.* You can do this for other parts of your body. If you do not feel like saying out the statements, you can also follow a recorded session, which will prompt you.

In the next section, we will look at some additional techniques to reinforce the effectiveness of autogenic therapy, such as exercises on breathing, mindfulness, and guided imagery.

*Breathing*

Although mentioned above, breathing is more than mere inhalation and exhalation. Breathing improves your overall well-being and draws on the well of positivity that is inside of you. With your eyes closed, take a deep breath in through your nose, filling your lungs completely. Slowly exhale through your mouth, releasing all the air from your lungs. Pause for a few seconds before taking another deep breath in through your nose. Repeat this process for a few minutes, focusing on your breath and letting go of any distracting thoughts. This is especially beneficial before a stressful situation.

## Guided Imagery

This is meditating using an image or soothing scenery. You can either think of something from the past or use a painting or a photo to focus your attention on. Try to pick something which you can relate to or a theme you love. Then sit comfortably and try to imagine yourself in this place. The more details you can think of, the more authentic your experience will feel. This method is especially helpful for people who would like to reinforce a positive vision of themselves. This is also another powerful way of calming your mind when you feel the urge to get away from your reality.

## Mindfulness

This includes breathing and focusing your mind on the present. Any time you find your mind drifting, gently bring it back to the present moment. Initially, you may find it helpful to place an object in front of you to focus on, such as a candle. As you become more adept at it, you will find that you won't need a physical object to anchor your mind; you will simply be able to hold your mind "in place." This practice will be explained in more detail in the coming chapter.

## FROM PERSONAL EXPERIENCE

I used to be very impulsive when I was younger and got upset when things didn't go my way. I made spur-of-the-moment decisions that I would later regret. I once worked at a coffee shop and prided myself on providing great customer service. A new customer came in, and nothing I seemed to do would please her. Despite my best efforts, she left a poor review of me with my manager. My manager immediately sided with the customer and reprimanded me. I was furious that my manager didn't take my past work history into consideration, and I immediately quit my job. At the time, I was paying for my college education myself, and leaving my job wasn't a financially sound decision. If I hadn't acted impulsively, I would have continued working there until I found another job.

Much later, when I incorporated mindfulness and breathing techniques, I found that my emotional intelligence blossomed, and I was able to overcome challenges at work and in my personal life. The following is an exercise I still use when I find old habits popping up.

## BODY SCAN MEDITATION

Use the following instructions to gently ease yourself into a calm state of mind.

1. Lie or sit down in a comfortable position. Be sure not to fall asleep if you decide to lie down.

2. Take a few deep breaths and focus on your belly. Let it inflate and deflate like a balloon with every inhalation and exhalation. This deep and slow breathing is the main tool that you will use throughout this exercise.

3. Start with your head. Focus all your attention on your forehead region. If you feel any pressure or tightness there, try to release it so that you feel relaxed. If you have a headache, acknowledge it. Continue to breathe and imagine that with every exhalation, you are releasing a little of the pain. Keep doing it until you feel your pain subsiding.

4. Now proceed to each part of your body and repeat the above exercise—your neck; shoulders; upper arms, lower arms, and fingers; chest, back, and abdomen; your buttocks, thighs, calves, feet, and toes. Focus your attention, especially, on areas you feel are tight or rigid. Each time imagine releasing or letting go of your discomfort or pain as you exhale.

Over time, this exercise will help you relax and be at peace in your own skin.

## TAKEAWAYS

> *Emotions can get in the way or get you on the way.*
>
> — MAVIS MAZHURA

Do not allow emotions to rule your decisions, thoughts, and procrastinating behaviors. Instead, learn to own, control, and use them for your benefit.

Meanwhile, let's discover how a proactive mindset will bring many pieces of this book together.

# 8

# STEP 6—ADOPTING A PROACTIVE MINDSET TO REMOVE PROCRASTINATION

The sixth step of this journey requires you to put the steps you have already learned into place to design a proactive or growth mindset, taking charge of anything that is within your control and acknowledging what's not.

Here, we will differentiate between a "proactive" mindset, which means one where you will anticipate and prepare for anything, and a "reactive" mindset, wherein you deal with challenges as they come (Cooks-Campbell, 2022). Let us see which of these two is better for us to put an end to our overthinking, procrastinating, and ruminative tendencies.

## PROACTIVE VS. REACTIVE MINDSETS

Proactive behavior is when you anticipate what could happen and take measures to counter them right now. It involves acting upon future problems that could arise. It takes a little bit of forethought, and as it is grounded in planning, it helps you to stay better prepared, promotes stability and accountability, and saves time.

Reactive behavior is dealing with a problem when it arises. You react to the problem at hand. It has its own benefits, such as being able to bring more creativity to the table and taking things as they come. However, on the flip side, it involves little to no planning, and thus, it may take more time for you to solve problems.

Proactive thinking is what you've been preparing for since Step 1. You have created an organized flow using time management, which should allow for daily proactive training. Then, you set goals and priorities to help you plan for and anticipate how you will respond to potential problems. Remember, you can't predict every future challenge. But you can start preparing for the common ones, which you did in Steps 3, 4, and 5. Step 6 will guide you to prepare for future problems, eliminating the risk of missing opportunities and helping you cope with each dilemma better.

Let us now look at some tips related to being proactive:

- Surround yourself with positive people. It is difficult to jump into any positive venture and stay proactive if you have people pulling down your physical and mental energies. Therefore, choose your company wisely and keep those who are like-minded close, and disengage from negativity.
- Assume responsibility for your life, which includes past decisions, future opportunities, and possible mistakes. Ownership also means you must apply self-compassion and gratitude for what you have done right. Forgive yourself for the mistakes you have made and acknowledge your achievements.
- Commit to taking action on urgent and important priorities (Step 2). This is very vital to avoid procrastination and to ensure that you are moving forward. Keep progressing a little every day. It does not matter if the pace is slower than you imagined. Even crawling ahead is better than standing still.
- Start thinking with intention (some of which we covered under cognitive restructuring) and only make intentional decisions. We already talked about mindfulness and being completely present. Whatever choice you make, let it be wholly yours. Do not feel pressured or go with the flow only to

realize that you are headed somewhere you do not want to be.

- Focus your mental energy on what matters. Keep track of your goals and work toward them. Eliminate the unnecessary and make room only for things and people that matter to your well-being and success.
- Be mindful. You are the gatekeeper of your mind. Take charge of your thoughts, emotions, and feelings. The more you practice, the more in control you will be.
- Reevaluate your beliefs and know what they are. Your goals and priorities will inspire values. Using Step 7 in the next chapter, you will be able to hone your values by focusing on your true purpose and basic needs.

Now let us look at some of the above points in more detail, particularly at how they can be implemented in our lives.

### Surrounding Yourself With Positivity

There are several ways of doing this, starting with yourself and your thoughts and proceeding to your external surroundings.

**Use proactive affirmations to rewrite your internal dialogue**: You can keep a physical or digital journal for this. But the language you use is what matters at the end of the day. You have to reaffirm full faith and confidence in yourself, your ideas, thoughts, emotions, beliefs, dreams, and goals. I would suggest using "I" statements like the ones below:

- I manage all my decisions, because I am well-prepared.
- I act with purpose, ensuring things get done.
- I know I have choices. I make my choices.
- Whatever I do impacts my future; thus, I will make all my actions count.
- I am the person I always dreamed of becoming.

You can search online and use prompts for the affirmations you think would be most meaningful in your path forward.

**You become the company you keep:** How do you identify positive people? Keep a lookout for people who will help you achieve more. They will push you out of your comfort zone and encourage you to try out new things. They are happy, cheerful, and optimistic, despite things that go wrong. They take genuine pride in your accomplishments. They will also inspire generosity and gratitude in you. Why must you keep them close? These traits will eventually rub off on you, and this is what you aspire to become. So, let go of people who are toxic. Instead, welcome people who are self-motivated and successful into your life.

**Think of ways you can stay more positive:** The number one tip for this is to be mindfully present. Ninety-eight percent of stress is over things in the past or future. Keep those aside and instead focus on the present (Urquhart, n.d.). You can do this by first acknowledging the negative thought and then not engaging further with it. Do not analyze them or worry about them; just notice them and then set them aside. Next, search for a positive thought or picture and hold on to it. Try to inject the positivity that you find in this thought into your feelings. It will take some time, but with practice, you will find perpetuating positivity easier.

**Infuse humor:** There is nothing like something funny to cheer you up. So, find the lighter side of life. Yes, things go wrong. Sometimes, nothing you do seems to work out. Instead of fretting about it, laugh out loud. What can you laugh about? Just about anything. You can make yourself the butt of the joke. Laugh at life. Laugh at people whom you find to be a pain. Most importantly, just keep yourself entertained. As with being present in the moment, the more you train yourself to find humor, the more it will find you.

Now that we have looked at some ways to keep ourselves and the environment around us positive, let us look at some ways to take ownership of our life.

## Practicing Self-Compassion

**Self-compassion meditation:** This is a powerful tool to exercise self-compassion. You can start by selecting a place that is peaceful and quiet (Neff, 2019). Sit or lie down in a posture that you are comfortable in. Close your eyes, breathe in and out deeply, and pay attention to your body. Observe the minute things, such as how your clothes feel against your skin or the sensation of the mat or cushion on your back. How your toes rest on the floor or if you are lying down, how you can feel the coolness of the floor. You can also bring your attention to the sounds you can hear—the birds chirping or the traffic right outside. Now, breathe gently as you think of one incident or event that has been stressing you. Acknowledge that "this is a difficult moment." Breathe and then tell yourself deliberately, "I am not alone." Breathe again and then say the words, "May I find it within me to be kind to myself." Repeat these three statements as many times as you like and for as long as you like.

**Pen a letter to yourself:** Just as powerful as the self-compassion exercise, writing a letter to yourself is thera-peutic and can act like a safety valve for your emotions (Neff, 2019). Think of yourself as an extremely under-standing friend who can see into your mind and soul. Write a letter to yourself imagining you are this friend. Ensure you include points in the letter about your strengths as well as your weaknesses. Let your letter to yourself see you as a whole person, with the good, the bad, and the ugly. Accept yourself for who you are and see the beauty that lies in your being. Remind yourself that you are human and that despite mistakes you might have made, you deserve love, health, and happiness.

**Nonjudgmental Affirmations** (Moore, 2019): Tell yourself as often as you like that you, as a person, matter too. The following are some statements that you can try:

1. I am not bound to others' judgment of me.
2. It is okay to treat myself with kindness.
3. I accept who I am wholly.
4. I have made mistakes; I forgive myself for them.
5. I am trying to change. It is not easy, but I am trying, and it is easier if I am less harsh with myself.

### Mindfulness

The last component of a proactive mind is one that practices mindfulness, which we briefly touched upon in the last chapter too. Let us look at why being mindful is so transformative and some very simple tools to incorporate mindfulness into your daily lives.

There is science behind the practice of mindfulness meditation techniques. Kristoffer Rhoads, a psychologist at Harborview Medical Center (Boynton, 2020), tells us that mindfulness meditation can be extremely rejuvenating for the brain. It develops and activates several parts of the brain, including the gray matter and the hippocampus, which are associated with memory and cognition. He says that these changes in the brain can be mapped after a year or so of meditation. Second, meditation can calm down the sympathetic nervous system, the one that is in charge of the "flight-fight-freeze" reactions we mentioned earlier in the book. This is helpful in reducing stress, anxiety, pain, depression, and other negative emotions.

Below are some ways in which you can become more mindful every day, starting now (Pal et al., 2018).

- **Mindful waking and intentions:**

Wake up and set your intentions for the day. Just sit up in your bed and take three refreshing breaths and then say to yourself one simple intention. *I will be kind to myself* or *I will be considerate to others* are some statements you can pick from. Throughout the day, check in with yourself whether you are following your intention for the day.

- **Mindful eating:**

Whenever you have meals, be fully present. Do not scroll through your phone or emails or the newspaper. Take in a couple of deep breaths and try to gauge how hungry you are on a scale of 1–10. It does not matter when you ate last. When you eat, enjoy every morsel, and notice the smell and texture and taste of the food. Most importantly, eat in proportion to your hunger.

- **Mindful workouts:**

Whatever form of exercise you choose, whether it is gardening or weight training, be intentional about your short- and long-term goal. For example, "I am going to work out for half an hour because I want to lose weight, get fitter, or because it makes me happy." Spend the first five minutes warming up with deep breaths and relaxing the different parts of your body. In the next quarter of an hour, build up the intensity of whatever you are engaged in, but settle down into a rhythm. For five minutes or so, challenge yourself so that you can reach the peak of exertion. Then give your body five minutes of cool down time, and finally rest for five minutes.

- **Mindful driving:**

Before you start, take a deep breath and begin by acknowledging where you want to go. As you drive, ask yourself what you need. Perhaps you feel a little tense and want a pep talk. Give yourself a pep talk and tell yourself you are safe, happy, and at ease. Look around and understand that most other drivers also want the same things as you, i.e., to travel safely, easily, and happily. Chant the words, "May we all be safe, at ease, and happy traveling these roads." Continue to breathe and be in tune with all your senses.

- **Mindful meditation:**

We already mentioned body scan meditation in the previous chapter. Additionally, you can also practice sitting or walking meditation whenever and wherever you want in the day. With your feet flat on the floor and your hands on your lap, make yourself comfortable in a seat. Focus on how your breath enters and exits your body while breathing through your nose. If ideas or bodily sensations disrupt your meditation, take note of them, and then turn your attention back to your breathing.

Alternatively, find a peaceful area that is ten to twenty feet long, then walk slowly. Pay attention to the sensations of standing and the small movements that help you maintain balance as you walk. When your path comes to an end, turn around and keep walking while staying mindful of your feelings.

The practice of mindfulness is not limited to these techniques. There are many other ways to cultivate mindfulness in daily life. Find one that is right for you.

## FROM PERSONAL EXPERIENCE

Here's a simplified explanation of a unique coping technique I've developed over the years. It involves a kind of self-dialogue that might remind you of the way you talked to yourself as a child:

"C'mon, let's make a deal. If you help me complete this task, I'll treat you to some candy." - This is a way of encouraging and rewarding myself to get things done.

"Okay, let's put this scary thought on the shelf for a moment." - This strategy allows me to delay dealing with a stressful idea until I feel ready to handle it.

"Did something upset you? It's okay to feel sad but remember that everything will be okay." - This is how I comfort myself when I'm feeling down.

"You seem tired. Why don't you take a break and rest?" - This is how I remind myself to take care of my physical well-being, acknowledging the importance of rest.

"Even though things are messy right now, I still love and value you." - This is a way of expressing self-compassion and acceptance, even when things aren't going perfectly.

While it might sound a little odd, this approach has truly helped me. Combined with the practice of mindfulness and introspective techniques, it has been an essential tool in mastering my mind. Over time, this practice has made me much more proactive, enabling me to effectively manage my thoughts and reactions.

## GRATITUDE JOURNAL

Gratitude is an emotion that can bring you a lot of joy and purpose. I have always had a special journal in which I scribble away all the things that I am happy and grateful for. It is an easy exercise requiring not more than fifteen minutes of your time daily. Here are a few tips to start your own gratitude journal.

1. Think of five things or people that inspire gratitude in you. Remember to keep your list short because you will be explaining a little bit about each of these.
2. Give specific details of why each item or person made it to your list.
3. Focus on the emotions each of those five evokes in you.
4. Try to imagine how not having these things or people would change your life.
5. Thank God or the universe or the cosmos for bringing these "gifts" to you.

Keep writing in your journal daily or as often as you can. Remember, you can write about the same people, events, or objects, but focus on a different aspect each time you write. You can also think of surprises or events out of the ordinary you are eternally grateful for.

## TAKEAWAYS

> To master the universe, first master your own mind.

— MEHMET M. ILDAN

Mastering your mind, becoming proactive, adopting a growth attitude, and becoming capable of making decisions and overcoming rumination requires time and patience.

However, with commitment, dedication, and practice, the results will shine bright. Next, let us discover the purpose of working your way through these steps in the next chapter.

# 9

# STEP 7—FINDING YOUR IKIGAI WITH MASLOW'S HIERARCHY OF NEEDS

Step seven is about finding your true potential to improve every aspect of your life, including how you think about things, behave, and feel about and react to specific situations. Moreover, the entire theory is based on your basic human needs. So, why aren't you utilizing your *ikigai* to promote your well-being and stop rumination, overthinking, and procrastination? Finding your ikigai will help you make better decisions and trump your perfectionism by allowing you to be your best self.

You have to meet your own needs first before becoming your best self (Llego, 2022). Organizing your life and schedule, setting goals, changing thought patterns, and overcoming the consequences of rumination and perfectionistic ideations require you to set your core values, which align with your full potential, purpose, and best self.

## SELF-ACTUALIZATION

Self-actualization can look different for different people, and not everyone achieves it. In Abraham Maslow's Hierarchy of Needs Theory (which we are coming to shortly), he says only one percent of the adult population attains this final stage of development. Here, a person is able to reach the epitome of their potential but is aware of their self-barriers. In other words, they feel that they can use their talents fully, but are also realistically aware of how far they can go.

How do we measure self-actualization? In psychological terms, a person who has achieved their goals, practices self-acceptance, and assesses themselves in a realistic but optimistic manner can be called self-actualized.

### Maslow's Hierarchy of Needs

Maslow's Hierarchy (Selva, 2017) is a pyramid that establishes human needs from the most basic to the most sophisticated. At the base of the pyramid, he lists the physical needs we have, like food, clothing, warmth, and rest. At the next level, comes the safety and security needs, such as having a safe shelter. Right on top of that is our need for intimate and loving relationships such as family and friends. Once these three needs are taken care of, people need to feel respected for their accomplishments. This is why we feel the need to "perform" at our jobs. On top of this, comes the last and final need, self-actualization, where a person wants to work to their full potential and feel that their creative energies are used for something productive.

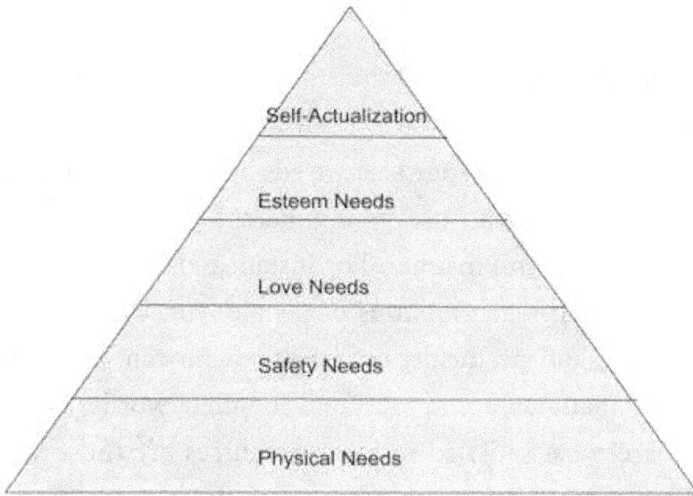

There are a couple of needs (*Self-Actualization*, 2019) that have to be realized for self-actualization. We need to understand these before we proceed to how we achieve it. These include

- being able to accept facts
- possessing problem-solving skills
- employing a firm moral compass
- being impartial
- using creativity
- being spontaneous

As is clear from the list above, self-actualization requires a person to be mature in their understanding of their surroundings, to use their creativity and spontaneity in solving problems. They also need to have a rational belief system in place and be unprejudiced in the decisions they make about people and situations.

Self-actualization is an important part of mental well-being (Selva, 2017). If you are self-actualized, you are able to fulfill not just all your basic needs but also your need to be respected and to use your inherent gifts in a meaningful and fruitful manner. For instance, think of a musician who can reach millions of people with the songs he composes and performs; or a writer who can touch the lives of many and is appreciated for their words. People who are most satisfied in jobs or courses are those who are self-actualized or able to use their aptitude to the fullest in achieving their goals. Nurturing "genius" is vital for self-actualization.

One of the most important habits of a self-actualized person is their focus on the journey rather than the goal. In other words, they undertake a mission not because they want to reach a specific point, but because they feel accomplished by just being a part of it. For instance, ask yourself, *why do you study?* If your answer is a variant of *to get good marks, to pass the exam,* or *to complete the course,* then that is not the true hallmark of self-actualization. But if your answer sounds something like, *I would like to learn more about this to satisfy my curiosity*, then that answer counts toward self-actualization.

Closely related to the above is the concept of a "sense of purpose" that people so often talk about. What you do must hold a certain value for you personally. Think of your job. Why do you do it? Yes, we all need money. And I am in no way denying the value of financial security. We need money to live—for food, education, a home, fuel for transportation, etc. But if your job only serves the function of providing you with money, then you could be deeply unsatisfied with what you are doing. Think of the things you love doing—it could be curating art, writing, or even helping people. Now, imagine if this "love" of yours could be integrated into your work, which would also pay your bills. How much happier would you feel at work? This, in a nutshell, is your "sense of purpose." Self-actualization must include a sense of purpose so that the answers to the questions—Are you where you are supposed to be? and Are you happy doing what you are doing? are both the same—a resounding "Yes!" This sense of purpose is what the Japanese call ikigai, the true reason for living (Hughes, 2021). We will come back to ikigai in the next section.

Self-actualization can be a lot of things. But it is not perfectionism. Overthinkers generally tend to have this latter trait in such abundance that we sometimes find it hard to set about a task simply because we are not sure if it will turn out to be the best possible thing we can do. Thus, in order to be self-actualized, we need to let go of this burden of perfectionism. The self-actualized are independent and are fearless to try out new things, even if they are not the best at what they do. In fact, they will know realistically where they stand, and this will encourage them, in turn, to convert their talents into something unique. For example, suppose you start writing. You know you are not the best writer out there, but you keep honing your skills and publishing short pieces on your blog. Some of them are ignored, others are criticized, but one day you hit upon what you can do with your skill. You realize that when you give personal advice, connecting them with your own experiences, people are not just reading but also sharing your work. If you had not written anything, thinking of yourself as an average writer, you would never have gained this following!

The following are some of the attributes of a self-actualized person (*Self-Actualization*, 2019):

- accepts oneself and other people
- upholds meaningful and deep connections
- shows compassion and empathy for others
- has an accurate perception of reality in relation to oneself and others
- possesses a sense of humor, especially the capacity to laugh at one's own errors
- is creative, sometimes called a "creative spirit"

- has a sense of purpose and carries out consistent actions that further that aim
- seeks out special, happy moments in life—what Maslow called "peak experiences"
- has a constant appreciation for life's goodness—a quality often referred to as "childlike wonder"

When you are self-actualized you can see the "big picture," and you can work toward that with all your heart and soul, knowing that your authenticity to yourself and others rests in it. This work that you put in will also ultimately help you grow as a person.

## IKIGAI

Ikigai is your reason for living life or your purpose in life. "Iki" in Japanese means life, and "gai" is value, reason, or worth (Hughes, 2021). As a concept, it dates back to the Heian Period between the eighth and twelfth century. As far as Maslow's self-actualization goes, ikigai is the part where you find your reason for getting out of bed every day. Ikigai has been broken down into its four constituent elements for ease's sake. In other words, to find your ikigai, you'd have to find the meeting point of the below:

- **Your passion:** What do you love doing?
- **Your strength:** What are you good at?
- **The talent you can monetize:** What can you be paid for?

- **Your contribution to the world:** What do you think the world needs?

Ikigai matters because it defines your satisfaction with yourself and the world around you. It will help you forge deep bonds with the people that surround you. Ikigai can give you the balance you seek—inside and outside of you. More than everything else, your love for life is determined by how well you recognize and pursue your ikigai.

How can you find your ikigai? There are a couple of tools that you can use to measure and seek your ikigai. First, let us use this simple tool called "Ikigai-9" translated from Japanese into English by ikigai experts Yasuhiro Kotera and Dean Fido, to measure your ikigai.

1. I often feel that I am happy.
2. I would like to learn something new or start something.
3. I feel that I am contributing to someone or the society.
4. I have room in my mind.
5. I am interested in many things.
6. I think that my existence is needed by something or someone.
7. My life is mentally rich and fulfilled.
8. I would like to develop myself.
9. I believe that I have some impact on someone. (Sutton, 2021).

Now read the statements again and score yourself for each of them between 1–5, where 1 stands for "does not apply to me at all" and 5 stands for "applies to me a lot." Add up your scores for all nine questions, and you should get a score out of forty-five. You can use the following key to measure your ikigai:

| | |
|---|---|
| 38–45 | Extremely satisfied |
| 33–38 | Satisfied |
| 27–33 | Slightly satisfied |
| 25 | Neutral |
| 19–24 | Slightly dissatisfied |
| 12–18 | Dissatisfied |
| 9–11 | Extremely dissatisfied |

To find your ikigai, ask yourself the following questions:

- What was your favorite hobby as a child?
- What is your favorite hobby now?
- What do people usually turn to you for help?
- What would you consider your strengths or skills?
- What could you sell? (It could be a product/service/skill)
- What profession or job would suit you?
- What do you want to leave as your legacy?
- What would you like to change about the world?

Now, take all the answers you get and try to work out where your ikigai lies. Remember, this is a very individualized process. You can revisit the questions if you get stuck, but your answers have to be honest and accurate.

Positive Psychology (Sutton, 2021) provides you with several tools and worksheets to find your ikigai. You can use them to refine your search for ikigai.

Next, we look at a few pointers on how you can expand your vision so that searching for your ikigai will not be as daunting and laborious a task as it would be otherwise:

- **Read:** Read as many books as you can. Research suggests that reading even spiritual texts and novels can give people a sense of purpose (Smith, 2018). A lot of what we see and experience is shaped by ideas we pick up from books. Thus, it is important to just keep reading so that you can give form to your unspoken thoughts and feelings.
- **Volunteer:** Donate your time, expertise, or money to causes. It is not just an avenue to meet others, but also a space to develop the "gift of giving." You can choose charities or social service programs you really care about. Or it can be simply an experiment.
- **Ask for feedback:** Whether it is from your parents, teachers, siblings, close friends, colleagues, or significant other, ask for feedback on your work, opinions, ideas, and on things or areas you love. These people who know you will be able to give you certain ideas on areas you may

have missed. This will help clarify things such as what you should do next, where you should go, or whom to meet to realize your ikigai.

- **Develop humanitarianism and gratitude:** In every situation, be helpful. See how you can make a change in the life of a person around you. Be grateful for all the things you have, and in turn, be the instrument to evoke this gratitude in people around you. Studies show that generosity and benevolence can be great drivers of self-actualization (Smith, 2018). In another study, researchers found that while happiness was linked to giving or taking, finding meaning in life was linked more to giving (Morin, 2022).

- **Surround yourself with like-minded people:** The people you keep close can mend or mar your relationship with your ikigai. Choose people who are encouraging, kind, thoughtful, wise, and honest with you. If you need you to matter out there, then your close allies must push you to do more, not extinguish your spark.

- **Explore your interests:** Forget what you may or may not be good at. When given an opportunity, do things that make you uncomfortable or let you explore skills you have never used yet. The more things you do, the more you will understand where your happiness truly lies, and the easier it will be for you to find your ikigai. Or rather, your ikigai may just come and find you.

## CORE VALUES

There are a set of five broad core values that most people have. These are:

- **Honesty:** Doing and saying things that are right.
- **Esteem:** Treating others and yourself with respect.
- **Responsibility:** Taking ownership of your duties.
- **Sportsmanship:** Being fair-minded and playing by the rules.
- **Leadership/ Service mindedness:** Willing to lead or serve people and giving back to your community.

But we need to be more in control of the core values we possess so that we have agency over what we allow for ourselves, in terms of thoughts, and emotions, and what we do not. The following seven steps will guide you through how to achieve this.

1. **Embrace a growth mindset:** Starting with the right mental attitude is half the battle won. You must think of yourself as a novice, willing to learn on the journey. Take a deep breath and keep your mind clear for this learning to come.
2. **List your personal values:** Do not take the easy way of simply "compiling" a list. Instead, take your time and "create" it. Do not use ready-made

personal values available on the internet or from other sources. Instead, ponder what is important to you.

3. **Categorize your personal values into groups:** Once you have your list above, some of these values might be related to each other. Group them by their similarities. For instance, accountability and responsibility could be grouped together.

4. **Highlight the dominant values in each group:** Once you have grouped your personal values, highlight the most important one or the one that could describe all the others as the predominant value. Keep the rest bulleted under this main point.

5. **Identify your top core values:** You may still find a sizable number of values in your hands. This will make putting them into action difficult. Again, sort them so that you arrive at five to ten values that are most important to you personally. You must also try to rank them in order of their importance to you.

6. **Enrich your personal values:** Make your personal values more meaningful to you by adding your personal stories, using slightly richer vocabulary, or creating value statements that stand out for you. This is so that your mind can hold onto them for longer.

7. **Commit to your values:** In this last step, ask yourself whether each of your values is in keeping

with who you are and what you stand for. Is the ranking of your values as it should be? Most importantly, how do your core values make you feel? Do they contribute to making you unique?

## FROM PERSONAL EXPERIENCE

I struggled to find purpose in my life. I did odd jobs that helped me with paying my bills, but none of them really fired me up. A corporate job I landed looked glamorous on the outside, and initially, I was thrilled with the salary and the corporate culture. But after a while, the novelty and the enchantment wore off. I was overworked, stressed, constantly on my toes, and yet felt dissatisfied. What bothered me most was that I was a cog in the larger process. If I were to fall down dead at my job, I would merely be replaced by another like me. None of my inherent skill sets or talents were either recognized or utilized. I felt like a machine on most days, just completing my tasks and getting out of the office for a breath of fresh air.

Finally, a combination of wellness challenges and mental health struggles made even the paycheck seem not worth the effort I was putting in to sustain my lifestyle. I quit and engaged in things I enjoyed. For instance, I enrolled in an art class, creative writing workshops, mental wellness, and art of living courses. Suddenly, I discovered I wasn't tied to any one thing, that I still had time to do many things, and to make my mark in the world by experimenting with many roles. I even learned to use some of these new-found skills to help others and make enough money to pay my bills. I still am a Jack of many trades today, and yet I feel happier than I ever was because everything I do contributes to my ikigai and my core values.

## QUESTIONS TO PONDER

Here is a set of interesting (perhaps "bizarre" describes them better) questions I put together for myself to find my true inner purpose. I hope you have a laugh over it, but that it also helps you answer a few questions about yourself.

1. What is your definition of a shitshow? (Up to what level of crap are you willing to tolerate to maintain your status quo? Rank it if you want on a scale of 1–10)
2. How can you make a better fool of yourself? (What is the one thing that scares you, or something you are too shy to try, fearing public humiliation?)
3. What about you today would make the child in you cry? (How much have you deviated from your childhood dreams?)

4. What makes you forget to eat and sleep? (What activity makes you hold your attention like no other?)

5. What's your superpower? (How can you help people, given your skills?)

6. Gun to your head, if you were forced to leave your house and be at a place every single day of your life, where would you choose to go? (How or where would you love to spend your time?)

7. If you knew you would die a year from today, what is one thing you would do to be remembered? (What will you leave as your legacy?)

Answer the previous questions, and then use the other tools provided in this chapter to step closer to your ikigai and sense of purpose.

## TAKEAWAYS

> *With nothing meaningful in life, nothing is interesting. Enter boredom. A bored woman even longs for longing. She has time to fill, but there's nothing compelling to do.*
>
> — DANIEL KLEIN

Find your ikigai and pursue self-actualization if you want true meaning without the false pursuit of perfectionism. You have completed the steps to embrace a new mind, life, and meaning. But wait, there is one last step left. It is time to discover how to face your greatest fears during your journey.

# 10

# STEP 8—USING GESTALT PSYCHOLOGY TO REDUCE DISSONANCE AND FEAR

S tep eight is an unusual one many avoid discussing because facing fear head-on is a trigger for anxiety. That is why you will need Gestalt's famous psychological theory to overcome extreme fears related to changing your thoughts, becoming emotionally intelligent, or ending procrastination to start something new.

Fear is an extremely powerful emotion that might cause you to return to overthinking, procrastination, rumination, poor decisions, and pursuing perfection (Clapp, n.d.). Fear is your foe, and in most cases, it results in an irrational response. So, let's take care of it once and for all.

## FEAR AS A PART OF COGNITIVE DISSONANCE

Fear is a natural part of cognitive dissonance. We say that one of the biggest shapers of human experience is the fear of the unknown. It is the same when we try anything new —getting into a new relationship, trying out a new workout regimen, or even when you quit a job or find a new one. The following are some negative ways in which fear stemming from cognitive dissonance can affect us:

- overstaying at jobs, in toxic relationships
- placing blame on things and people around you rather than accepting it
- distortion of truths or outright lies to find comfort in situations
- defending abusive people

Cognitive dissonance can also manifest in other ways than fear, and those would look like the below:

- avoidance of confrontation
- squeamishness about talking about what seems fair to you
- ignoring facts in order to fit the situation or person into your perception of them
- rationalization of things that are wrong
- fear of missing out (FOMO)
- a sense of shame about yourself
- guilt about not being able to do anything right

So, how can you handle this fear? Let us look at the main tool to tackle fear in the next section.

## GESTALT THERAPY

Gestalt therapy is a relatively new approach, which originated in Austria and Germany in the twentieth century. It aims to understand your perception and create a whole conception from a fragmented understanding of a situation. It proposes that the whole of a situation is different from the sum of its parts (The Editors of Encyclopaedia, 1998).

The main principles of Gestalt therapy (Cherry, 2022c) are:

- **Prägnanz:** People generally tend to understand things in their simplest forms.
- **Similarity:** We tend to form associations between people, places, and things based on their properties. For instance, we group people by their size, their ethnicity, or the color of their hair, etc.
- **Proximity:** Objects that are near each other are often grouped together in our minds.
- **Continuity:** Things, places, or events in a line or curve are often associated with one another, while things removed from this curve are not placed with them.

- **Closure:** We often link the missing pieces of a situation to fill in the blanks or to make sense of it. In practical terms, this is how we might read a piece of paper with instructions on them, even if a small piece of it is torn and missing. In relationships, we ascribe meanings to a person's actions or words from the past even when we no longer have any connection with or access to the person.

- **Common region:** Objects in a common place are often associated with each other. For instance, things in a box, even if dissimilar, are often grouped together by our minds.

Gestalt theory can help us focus on the present rather than trying to analyze the individual episodes from our past. Though Gestalt theory recognizes the importance of past events as a whole in shaping human personality, it does not encourage us to scrutinize each episode, person, or thing from our past. The focus always remains on the present.

In everyday language, how can Gestalt therapy help you combat your fears then? Gestalt therapy will help you see events, incidents, people, and objects as part of a whole rather than as individual pieces of a puzzle. In short, you will be able to complete the jigsaw puzzle to see everything as part of the bigger picture. Emotions, thoughts, beliefs, and actions no longer seem separate, but are one true experience.

So, how can you use Gestalt theory to your advantage in fighting anxiety, panic, stress, and fear? Dissonance is a process of fragmentation. Therefore, you must pull these various strands of thoughts or emotions together before trying to change the whole. You have already started working on them individually with CBT for thought processing and changing beliefs and when you began practicing rational emotive therapy. Now, all that remains is for you to put them all back together again. However, fear is a challenging sum to remove from the rest because it quickly puts your dissonance in overdrive, causing it to retaliate and make the situation fragmented again.

Let us now look at some specific Gestalt techniques (Shoreline Recovery, 2021). You must also realize that some of these techniques may require guidance from a professional for you to be able to reap the best results from them.

### The Empty Chair

Think of what you would tell yourself from another period of your life. What advice, from your perspective now, would you give to that version of you? How would you ask yourself to cope with whatever you were struggling with at that time? What would you say to comfort that version of you?

Now, place an empty chair before you and imagine that you from that period of struggle is seated there. Talk to yourself, holding a conversation about your deepest, darkest fears from then. Allay your fears and comfort yourself in the light of what you know to be true today.

### Creative Art

One of the best methods employed by Gestalt methodology is to use art as an outlet for unspent emotions. In fact, it can help you come to terms with yourself better. For instance, you can paint, draw, or sculpt to stay more in touch with your surroundings and to process things that happen around you. The therapeutic effect of art is quite recognized by psychology today.

### Role Play

This is very similar to the empty chair method. You will essentially speak to a version of yourself. Depending on your personality, there might be dominant and submissive parts of your nature, all of which will find a voice through this exercise.

### Exaggeration

You can use self-expression, such as exaggerated motions or facial expressions, to act out a certain episode. This will help you recall the details. This will also help in relating an emotion to a specific incident, especially if the said emotion has been suppressed over time. For instance, say you were very angry with a friend for a particular reason but never had the opportunity to react as you should have; exaggeration will help you reenact the scene, but this time with an outlet for your true emotions. You may be asked to shout out or to express the sentiments you could only carry around in your system for so long.

### Emotion Location

A continuation of the above experience, you will be able to locate and connect your emotion to an incident. Certain traumatic episodes can cause people to delink from their emotions completely. Emotion location will help you place your emotions back into the equation in a safe manner so that your feelings are acknowledged and validated. This will help you to transition out of negative thoughts about your past in an easier manner and move past them.

Now, we shall also look at some additional methods of dealing with your fear in the next section.

## ADDITIONAL FEAR MANAGEMENT TECHNIQUES

- **Pause:** Put some distance or time between yourself and your action when you experience fear. This will help you not react immediately to the situation and complicate it further.
- **Breathe:** We already discussed a breathing technique in Chapter 7. You can use this same technique to calm your mind when you feel scared.
- **Observe:** You can choose to sit in your fear and observe it for a while. This will help you identify the root cause of this sentiment.
- **Imagine the worst:** What is the worst that can happen if your fears were to come true? Sometimes, the consequences are lesser than what your mind makes it out to be.
- **Place fact against fear:** Is there a rational fact supporting your fear, or does it stem more from your emotional response to a situation?
- **Do not aim for perfection:** When you are afraid, you tend to procrastinate an action until you can get it perfectly right. Do not do this. Aim to complete the action, even if it is not the best you can do.
- **Visualize:** Think of a happy place where you are calm and at ease. This can be your go-to mental

peace whenever you feel frightened. Similar to the guided imagery exercise, you can detail the place as elaborately as you want to make it seem as realistic as possible.

- **Talk to your fear:** This might seem exaggerated, but talking to your fears can often make them appear smaller and less severe. Say things like, "I feel you, but you are not helping me. So, I am going to ignore you for a while."
- **Goals to the rescue:** Think of your goals, and then think of what you would achieve if you did not let your fear govern you. Sometimes, your goals will help you snap out of your fear.
- **Failure is a part of the process:** Acknowledge that failure is a part of growth. It is not something to be ashamed of. Failure is proof that you tried something new, and therefore, it is something that teaches you what not to do as you try yet again.

The above techniques are fairly simple, with resources on them available readily. You can read more on how to defeat fear on the websites of famous personality coaches such as Tony Robbins and others.

## FROM PERSONAL EXPERIENCE

Being a perfectionist, I never used to show my vulnerabilities to people. They often thought of me as a matter-of-fact, smart, confident person, and only I knew how suffocating it was to fulfill these stereotypes of myself. When I had my low phases, and I could barely get things done, I would just keep away from people so that they wouldn't have to see me that way. I was also extremely scared of losing people who would see the "real me." This is also why I never talked about my fears or my downs with anyone.

But things changed when I decided to embrace my fears. I told a couple of my close friends exactly what I had been dealing with. And contrary to my beliefs, many of my friends not only appreciated my openness, but also made it a point to check on me and offer their help. Yes, there were a few casualties, but these "fair-weather" friends were ones I needed to lose so that I could grow. I have no regrets about them leaving anymore. I am glad I took the bull by its horns and accepted and worked on my fears and my mentality. It has made me a whole new person. A person I am proud to have created.

## DREAM JOURNAL

I briefly mentioned suppressed feelings a while ago. Repressed feelings are worse than suppressed ones. Suppression is when you admit your underlying feelings but do not act upon them. When you refuse to even admit your underlying feelings, it is called repression. For instance, when your friend does something to hurt you, which you subconsciously recognize as horrible. Yet when you refuse to even acknowledge your anger toward this friend, your anger is repressed.

A dream journal is just the tool to help you explore your repressed emotions. It will help you retrieve your emotional truth so that you can move past your silent inner trauma. To do this, keep a journal recording your dreams using the following steps (MasterClass, 2021):

1. Write down your dream as accurately and realistically as it occurred. You have to capture it before you forget, and the sooner you can write it down, the easier it will be to get the details correct. Keep a pen and notepad at hand so that your dream does not slip away.
2. Write your dream in the present tense, giving it a sense of urgency and power that the past tense does not possess. It will also help you trace the narrative, flow of events, and the people in your dream better.
3. Aim for an emotional retelling rather than just a precise statement of facts. Since the main aim of this exercise is for emotional release, if you treat this as a fact-mining tool, it may not help. Instead, dig out the emotions you felt.
4. Track your sleep cycle. Scientifically speaking, you dream most during the Rapid Eye Movement (REM) phase of your sleep. Thus, if you keep track of your dreams, you will also get an idea of how

often you move through your sleep cycles and whether they are normal.

Now, use the above pointers to keep a record of your dreams. Are there familiar settings and timelines, or people they take you back to? Is there an emotion or energy from that space that you should acknowledge now for you to step out of your mental blocks? These are just two questions that will help you figure out what your mind is repressing.

## TAKEAWAYS

> *Facing it, always facing it. That is the way to get through. Face it!*
>
> — CONRAD JOSEPH

Facing your fears and seeing them as sums of a whole rather than as your standard response is how you overcome them. It is how you successfully burst the cognitive dissonance bubble. Ultimately, your success lies in how you complete the final step of ending overthinking patterns and rumination to become your best self.

# CONCLUSION

I hope *Overthinking Override* has given you a concrete plan of action toward taking destiny into your own hands. This book was born from the painstaking effort, research, and practice of laying down systematic tools to combat rumination, fear paralysis, and everything in between.

To recap, the main subjects we covered were:

- The scientific reasons behind why you overthink and ruminate.
- Identifying the common cognitive distortions that cause overthinking.
- Utilizing David Allen's system to organize lives and thoughts.
- Using Eisenhower's technique to prioritize things and setting GROW or SMART goals.

- Employing CBT exercises and worksheets to reframe thoughts and beliefs.
- Using RET to reconstruct emotions and make the right decisions.
- Applying the art of autogenic training and using emotional intelligence.
- Engaging in a proactive mindset for growth, overcoming procrastination, and stopping rumination.
- Finding ikigai to achieve self-actualization and override perfectionism.
- Applying Gestalt therapy to master fear and keep moving.

Let me share a transformational story with you. Once upon a time, a woman found herself tangled in a web of incessant thoughts. Now, thinking is natural, but her case was different. Her thoughts were invasive, obstructing her decisions and actions, and casting a shadow over both her professional and personal life. Her mind painted dark images, focusing on possible obstacles and problems that others seemed blissfully unaware of. With her mental landscape crowded with potential disasters, she had little energy or space left to take action.

But she realized that this state of paralysis couldn't be her destiny. So, she crafted a strategy, a set of techniques designed to navigate through her stormy thoughts. A few months later, she found a stranger looking back at her in the mirror. This stranger was confident, quick-thinking, decisive. The transformation extended to her relationships, affecting her connections with family, friends, and romantic partners. She developed a clear vision of what she wanted from life. Finally, she could enjoy life's lighter moments and sleep peacefully, no longer haunted by fear, procrastination, and missed opportunities.

The woman in the story is me. From the ashes of a broken past, I rose, like a phoenix, to rebuild my life. Looking back, I see my former self with gratitude. That version of me, that cycle of overthinking, was the catalyst that spurred my transformation and birthed this book, 'Overthinking Override.' It's my way of reaching out to people trapped in the silent struggle against their thoughts, like I once was.

Change might not come quickly or easily. It will require patience, time, and perhaps a level of mental conditioning you've never experienced before. But once you start to see the results, once you start living without being hamstrung by overthinking or the futile pursuit of perfection, you'll want nothing less.

# REFERENCES

Ackerman, C. E. (2017a, March 20). *CBT techniques: 25 cognitive behavioral therapy worksheets*. PositivePsychology.com. https://positivepsychology.com/cbt-cognitive-behavioral-therapy-techniques-worksheets/#cbt-tools:%7E:text=1.%20Journaling

Ackerman, C. E. (2017b, September 29). *Cognitive distortions: 22 examples & worksheets (& PDF)*. Positive Psychology. https://positivepsychology.com/cognitive-distortions/#common-cognitive-distortions

Ackerman, C. E. (2018, February 12). *Cognitive Restructuring Techniques for Reframing Thoughts*. Positive Psychology. https://positivepsychology.com/cbt-cognitive-restructuring-cognitive-distortions/#definition-cognitive-restructuring:

Ackerman, C. E. (2020, January 19). *5 REBT techniques, exercises and worksheets*. Positive Psychology. https://positivepsychology.com/rebt-techniques-exercises-worksheets/

Antonio, C. (2016, May 31). *6 ways to control your emotions and make better decisions*. Idealist. https://www.idealist.org/en/careers/6-ways-to-control-your-emotions-and-make-better-decisions#:

*Autogenic Training*. (2016, September 23). Good Therapy. https://www.goodtherapy.org/learn-about-therapy/types/autogenic-training#

Boynton, E. (2020, October 26). *What happens in the brain during meditation?*. Right as Rain by UW Medicine. https://rightasrain.uwmedicine.org/mind/well-being/science-behind-meditation#:

Buckner R. L. (2013). The brain's default network: origins and implications for the study of psychosis. *Dialogues in clinical neuroscience*, 15(3), 351–358. https://doi.org/10.31887/DCNS.2013.15.3/rbuckner

*Can mindfulness exercises help me?* (n.d.). Mayo Clinic. Retrieved April 27, 2023, from https://www.mayoclinic.org/healthy-lifestyle/consumer-health/in-depth/mindfulness-exercises/art-20046356#:

Capper, J. (2018, October 24). *Don't let negative thoughts sabotage your goals*. Healthy Place. https://www.healthyplace.com/blogs/mental healthforthedigitalgeneration/2018/10/dont-let-negative-thoughts-sabotage-your-goals#

Casino, C. (n.d.). *Negative thoughts quotes (164 quotes)*. Goodreads. Retrieved April 21, 2023, from https://www.goodreads.com/quotes/tag/negative-thoughts#:

Cherry, K. (2022a, November 7). *Cognitive dissonance and ways to resolve it*. Verywell Mind. https://www.verywellmind.com/what-is-cognitive-dissonance-2795012#:%7E

Cherry, K. (2022b, November 7). *How emotionally intelligent are you?*. Verywell Mind. https://www.verywellmind.com/what-is-emotional-intelligence-2795423#:%7E

Cherry, K. (2022c, November 8). *What is the gestalt approach in psychology?*. Verywell Mind. https://www.verywellmind.com/what-is-gestalt-psychology-2795808#:%7E

Cherry, K. (2023, February 22). *What does it mean to be self-actualized.* Verywell Mind. https://www.verywellmind.com/characteristics-of-self-actualized-people-2795963#:%7E

*Chronic stress puts your health at risk*. (2021, July 8). Mayo Clinic. https://www.mayoclinic.org/healthy-lifestyle/stress-management/in-depth/stress/art-20046037#:%7E

Chu, B., Marwaha, K., Sanvictores, T., & Ayers, D. (2022). *Physiology, Stress Reaction*. PubMed; StatPearls Publishing. https://www.ncbi.nlm.nih.gov/books/NBK541120/#:%7E

Clapp, R. (n.d.). *10 reasons why fear is so powerful in our lives*. Beyond Survival. Retrieved April 30, 2023, from https://beyondsurvival.org/blog/10-reasons-why-fear-is-so-powerful#:%7E

Classroom Mental Health. (n.d. a). *Helping students connect the dots: thoughts, feelings, & behaviors*. Classroom Mental Health - A Teacher's Toolkit for High School. https://classroommentalhealth.org/in-class/thoughts/#:%7E

Classroom Mental Health. (n.d. b). *Identifying automatic thoughts-feeling worksheet*. Classroom Mental Health - A Teacher's Toolkit for High School. Retrieved April 21, 2023, from https://classroommentalhealth.org/exercises/materials/identifying-automatic-thoughts/thought-feeling.pdf

Clear, J. (2014, April 7). *How to be more productive and eliminate time wasting activities by using the "Eisenhower box."* James Clear. https://jamesclear.com/eisenhower-box#:%7E

*Cognitive distortion.* (n.d.). APA Dictionary of Psychology. https://dictionary.apa.org/cognitive-distortion

*Cognitive Distortions Test.* (n.d.). IDRLabs. Retrieved April 17, 2023, from https://www.idrlabs.com/cognitive-distortions/test.php

Cooks-Campbell, A. (2022, February 17). *Reactive vs. proactive management styles: which one gets results?.* Better Up. https://www.betterup.com/blog/reactive-vs-proactive#:%7E

Denniston, D. (2021, November 10). *7 signs you exhibit cognitive dissonance.* David Denniston, CFA. https://www.daviddenniston.com/blog/7-signs-you-exhibit-cognitive-dissonance

The Editors of Encyclopaedia Britannica. (1998). *Gestalt psychology: definition, founder, principles, & examples.* Encyclopaedia Britannica. https://www.britannica.com/science/Gestalt-psychology#:%7E

*Eisenhower matrix.* (n.d.). Product Plan. Retrieved April 20, 2023, from https://www.productplan.com/glossary/eisenhower-matrix/#:%7E

Engay, J. (n.d.). *Overthinking quotes (168 quotes).* Goodreads. Retrieved April 10, 2023, from https://www.goodreads.com/quotes/tag/overthinking#:%7E

Flow Wall. (2016, October 25). *Psychological benefits of organization.* Garage Organization & Renovation Tips. https://www.flowwall.com/blog/psychological-benefits-organization#:%7E

Franklin, B. (2021, October 22). *31 amazing quotes about being organized* (J. Hage, Ed.). Filling the Jars. https://www.fillingthejars.com/quotes-about-being-organized/#:%7E

Garman, C. (n.d.). *Proactive affirmations.* Affirm Your Life. Retrieved April 26, 2023, from http://affirmyourlife.blogspot.com/2009/08/proactive-affirmations.html#:%7E

Goleman, D. (2019, August 27). *Go with your gut: emotional intelligence and decision making.* LinkedIn. https://www.linkedin.com/pulse/go-your-gut-emotional-intelligence-decision-making-daniel-goleman/

Graham, A. (2022). *6 celebrities that practice mindfulness.* Fizzy Mag. https://fizzymag.com/articles/six-celebrities-that-practice-mindfulness

Gregoire, C. (2017, April 3). *This common mental shortcut can lead to bad decision-making.* HuffPost. https://www.huffpost.com/entry/psychology-mental-shortcuts-decision-making_n_58e26bfee4b0c777f7892021#:%7E

Hughes, M. (2021, August 13). *What's your ikigai? finding meaning in work and life* . Mind Tools Blog. https://www.mindtools.com/blog/whats-your-ikigai/

Huntington, C. (n.d.). *Cognitive distortions: definition, list, & examples.* The Berkeley Well-Being Institute. Retrieved April 15, 2023, from https://www.berkeleywellbeing.com/cognitive-distortions.html#:%7E

The Idioms. (n.d.). *Method to madness.* The Idioms. Retrieved April 17, 2023, from https://www.theidioms.com/method-to-madness/

Ildan, M. M. (n.d.). *Mastering The Mind Quotes (4 quotes).* Goodreads. Retrieved April 27, 2023, from https://www.goodreads.com/quotes/tag/mastering-the-mind#:%7E

Indeed Editorial Team. (2023, February 4). *Reactive vs. proactive behavior: what's the difference?.* Indeed. https://www.indeed.com/career-advice/career-development/reactive-vs-proactive#:%7E

Jeffrey, S. (2014, June 4). *7 steps to discovering your personal core values.* CEO Sage. https://scottjeffrey.com/personal-core-values/#STEP1Start_with_a_Beginners_Mind

Joseph, C. (n.d.). *Face your fears quotes (27 quotes).* Goodreads. Retrieved April 30, 2023, from https://www.goodreads.com/quotes/tag/face-your-fears#:%7E

Kashyap, N. (2022, July 5). *Cognitive dissonance: hypocrisy, changing facts, and the mind.* Verywell Health. https://www.verywellhealth.com/cognitive-dissonance-5248814#:%7E

Klein, D. (n.d.). *Meaningful Life Quotes.* Goodreads. Retrieved April 30, 2023, from https://www.goodreads.com/quotes/tag/meaningful-life#:%7E

Kwik Learning. (2020, March 17). *4 reasons why your brain likes organization.* Kwik Learning. https://kwiklearning.com/kwik-tips/4-reasons-why-your-brain-likes-organization/

Lapaas. (2021, January 11). *Allen's Input Processing Technique.* Lapaas

Digital. https://lapaas.com/allens-input-processing-technique/
#:%7E

Lindberg, S. (2019, November 22). *Autogenic training: what it is and how
to do it.* Healthline. https://www.healthline.com/health/mental-
health/autogenic-training

Lindsay, C. (2022, August 4). *What is gestalt therapy? techniques, effectiveness, and more.* Psych Central. https://psychcentral.com/health/
gestalt-therapy#techniques

Llego, M. A. (2022, August 29). *The benefits of achieving self-actualization.*
TeacherPH. https://www.teacherph.com/achieving-self-
actualization/

Locke, J. (n.d.). *28 emotional intelligence quotes that can help make emotions
work for you, instead of against* (J. Bariso, Ed.). Inc.Africa. Retrieved
April 25, 2023, from https://incafrica.com/library/justin-bariso-
28-emotional-intelligence-quotes-that-can-help-make-emotions-
work-for-you-instead-of-against-you#:%7E

Manson, M. (2014, September 18). *7 strange questions that help you find your
life purpose.* Mark Manson. https://markmanson.net/life-purpose

MasterClass. (2021, September 9). *How to keep a dream journal: 3 benefits
of dream journaling.* MasterClass. https://www.masterclass.com/arti
cles/how-to-keep-a-dream-journal#WjMpUsfl5xlBqaFsx2RIP:%7E

Mazhura, M. (n.d.). *28 emotional intelligence quotes that can help make
emotions work for you, instead of against* (J. Bariso, Ed.). Inc.Africa.
Retrieved April 25, 2023, from https://incafrica.com/library/justin-
bariso-28-emotional-intelligence-quotes-that-can-help-make-
emotions-work-for-you-instead-of-against-you#:%7E

McGregor, J. (2014, September 8). What neuroscience tells us about
getting organized. *Washington Post.* https://www.washingtonpost.
com/news/on-leadership/wp/2014/09/08/what-neuroscience-
tells-us-about-getting-organized/#:%7E

Mckay, B., & Mckay, K. (2019, September 24). *The rationality of
emotions.* The Art of Manliness. https://www.artofmanliness.com/
character/behavior/the-rationality-of-emotions/#:

McNaughton, A. (2017, March 14). *Rational vs. irrational emotions: what
am I telling myself?.* Symmetry Counseling. https://www.symme

trycounseling.com/uncategorized/rational-vs-irrational-emotions-telling/#:

Mind Tools. (2022). *The GROW model of coaching and mentoring.* MindTools. https://www.mindtools.com/an0fzpz/the-grow-model-of-coaching-and-mentoring

Morin, A. (2022, December 26). *7 ways to find more meaning and purpose in your life.* Verywell Mind. https://www.verywellmind.com/tips-for-finding-your-purpose-in-life-4164689#:%7E

NAIA. (n.d.). Five core values. National Association of Intercollegiate Athletics. Retrieved April 30, 2023, from https://www.naia.org/champions-of-character/five-core-values#:%7E

Neff, K. (2019). *Self-compassion exercises.* Self-Compassion. https://self-compassion.org/category/exercises/#exercises

NHS. (2023, January 4). *10 ways to fight your fears.* Health Scotland. https://www.nhsinform.scot/healthy-living/mental-wellbeing/fears-and-phobias/10-ways-to-fight-your-fears#:%7E

Pal, P., Hauck, C., Goldstein, E., Bobinet, K., & Bradley, C. (2018, August 27). *5 simple mindfulness practices for daily life.* Mindful. https://www.mindful.org/take-a-mindful-moment-5-simple-practices-for-daily-life/#:%7E

Pariser, E. (n.d.). *Dissonance quotes (32 quotes).* Goodreads. Retrieved April 21, 2023, from https://www.goodreads.com/quotes/tag/dissonance#:%7E

Perry, E. (2022, September 21). *What is the 2-minute rule? avoid procrastination quickly.* Better Up. https://www.betterup.com/blog/what-is-the-two-minute-rule#:%7E

Pietrangelo, A. (2020, March 29). *The effects of stress on your body.* Healthline. https://www.healthline.com/health/stress/effects-on-body

Pillans, R. (2021, September 13). *Three models to help you set goals.* Planet Consulting. https://planetconsulting.com.au/articles/three-models-to-help-you-set-goals/#:%7E

Prakash, N. (n.d.). *Overthinking quotes (168 quotes).* Goodreads. Retrieved April 23, 2023, from https://www.goodreads.com/quotes/tag/overthinking#:%7E

Psychology Compass. (2018, October 4). *4 ways emotional control boosts your decision making skills*. Psychology Compass. https://psychology compass.com/blog/decision-making-skills/#:%7E

Quote Investigator. (2014, December 16). *The person who never makes a mistake will never make anything*. Quote Investigator. https://quotein vestigator.com/2014/12/16/no-mistakes/

Raypole, C. (2018, September 13). *Rational emotive behavior therapy*. Healthline; Healthline Media. https://www.healthline.com/health/ rational-emotive-behavior-therapy

Raypole, C. (2020, February 27). *Self-actualization: what it is and how to achieve it*. Healthline. https://www.healthline.com/health/self-actualization#characteristics

Rebello, K., Moura, L. M., Pinaya, W. H. L., Rohde, L. A., & Sato, J. R. (2018). Default mode network maturation and environmental adversities during childhood. *Chronic stress (Thousand Oaks), 2*, 2470547018808295. https://doi.org/10.1177/2470547018808295

Reist, P. L. (2018, September 11). *How to be more proactive: seven ways to get out of your head and start living with intention today*. Art of Living (United States). https://www.artofliving.org/us-en/seven-ways-to-get-out-of-your-head#:%7E

Robbins, T. (n.d.). *10 top steps on how to overcome fear and achieve goals*. Tony Robbins. Retrieved April 30, 2023, from https://www.tonyrob bins.com/stories/unleash-the-power/overcoming-fear-in-5-steps/ #:%7E

Roeling, M. (2017, April 18). *Interesting facts why you should be organized*. Organized Transitions LLC. https://www.organizedtransitionsllc. com/interesting-facts-organized/#:%7E

Santilli, M. (2022, January 11). *How to stop overthinking: causes and ways to cope*. Forbes Health. https://www.forbes.com/health/mind/what-causes-overthinking-and-6-ways-to-stop/#:%7E

Scott, E. (2021, September 13). *Release tension with this targeted medita-tion technique*. Verywell Mind. https://www.verywellmind.com/ body-scan-meditation-why-and-how-3144782#:%7E

*Self–Actualization*. (2019, March 15). Goodtherapy. https://www. goodtherapy.org/learn-about-therapy/issues/self-actualization#:%7E

Selva, J. (2017, May 5). *What is self-actualization? Meaning, theory + exam-*

*ples.* Positive Psychology. https://positivepsychology.com/self-actu
alization/#theory-self-actualization:%7E

Sharma, S. (2021, August 17). *Why surround yourself with positive people?
How to do it?.* Calm Sage . https://www.calmsage.com/reasons-to-
surround-yourself-with-positive-people/

Shatz, I. (n.d.). *How to stop procrastinating: tips and techniques for overcoming procrastination.* Solving Procrastination. Retrieved April 20,
2023, from https://solvingprocrastination.com/how-to-stop-
procrastinating/#:%7E

Shoreline Recovery. (2021, October 15). *Gestalt therapy techniques examples.* Shoreline Recovery Center. https://www.shorelinerecoverycen
ter.com/gestalt-therapy-techniques-examples/#:%7E

Sicinski, A. (2009, August 20). *How to use the GROW model to set actionable goals.* IQ Matrix Blog. https://blog.iqmatrix.com/grow-model

Sivananda, S. (2021, June 14). At the speed of thought. *The Economic
Times.* https://economictimes.indiatimes.com/opinion/speaking-
tree/at-the-speed-of-thought/articleshow/83521529.cms#:%7E

Smith, J. A. (2018, January 10). *How to find your purpose in life.* Greater
Good. https://greatergood.berkeley.edu/article/item/
how_to_find_your_purpose_in_life#:%7E

Sparks, D. (2019, April 24). *Mayo mindfulness: try the 4 A's for stress relief.*
Mayo Clinic News Network. https://newsnetwork.mayoclinic.org/
discussion/mayo-mindfulness-try-the-4-as-for-stress-relief/#:%7E

Stangor, C., & Walinga, J. (2014). 8.1 Learning by association: classical
conditioning. *Introduction to Psychology - First Canadian Edition.*
https://opentextbc.ca/introductiontopsychology/chapter/7-1-learn
ing-by-association-classical-conditioning/#:%7E

*Stress effects on the body.* (2018). American Psychological Association.
https://www.apa.org/topics/stress/body

*Stress: signs, symptoms, management & prevention.* (2021, January 28).
Cleveland Clinic. https://my.clevelandclinic.org/health/arti-
cles/11874-stress#:%7E:text=Physical%20symptoms%20of

Sutton, J. (2020, July 1). *Goal-setting: 20 templates & worksheets for
achieving goals.* Positive Psychology. https://positivepsychology.
com/goal-setting-templates-worksheets/#:%7E

Sutton, J. (2021, January 24). *Finding your ikigai: 8 questionnaires and tests*. PositivePsychology.com. https://positivepsychology.com/ikigai-test-questionnaires/#:%7E

Team Asana. (2022, October 4). *The Eisenhower matrix: how to prioritize your to-do list*. Asana. https://asana.com/resources/eisenhower-matrix#:%7E

Twain, M. (n.d.). *Top 25 small steps quotes (of 89)*. A-Z Quotes. Retrieved April 21, 2023, from https://www.azquotes.com/quotes/topics/small-steps.html#:%7E

Tzeses, J. (2020, November 30). *Cognitive dissonance: what it is & why it matters*. Psycom. https://www.psycom.net/cognitive-dissonance

Urquhart, J. (n.d.). *What is the present moment & how does it bring you calm & joy?* Jody Urquhart. https://www.idoinspire.com/blog/what-is-the-present-moment-how-does-it-bring-you-calm-joy#:%7E

Villines, Z. (2019, October 21). *Cognitive dissonance: definition, effects, and examples*. Medical News Today. https://www.medicalnewstoday.com/articles/326738

Virtanen, A. (2022, October 4). *The magic of brain plasticity: why it's never too late to learn!* Growth Engineering. https://www.growthengineering.co.uk/brain-plasticity/#elementor-action

Williamson, N. (2019, September 26). *Stop procrastinating, read this story now*. Daily Maverick. https://www.dailymaverick.co.za/article/2019-09-27-stop-procrastinating-read-this-story-now/#:%7E